THE
FEMALE
MEMBER

Also by Kit Schwartz

THE MALE MEMBER

THE
FEMALE
MEMBER

*Being a Compendium
of Facts, Figures,
Foibles, and Anecdotes
about the Loving Organ*

Kit Schwartz

ST. MARTIN'S PRESS

NEW YORK

THE FEMALE MEMBER. Copyright © 1988 by Kit Schwartz.
All rights reserved.
Printed in the United States of America.
No part of this book may be used or reproduced
in any manner whatsoever without written permission
except in the case of brief quotations embodied
in critical articles or reviews.
For information, address St. Martin's Press,
175 Fifth Avenue, New York, N.Y. 10010.

Design by M. Paul

Library of Congress Cataloging-in-Publication Data

Schwartz, Kit.
    The female member / by Kit Schwartz.
        p.   cm.
    ISBN 0-312-01428-7 (pbk) : $8.95
    1. Vagina—Miscellanea.   2. Vagina—Anecdotes, facetiae,
satire, etc.   I. Title.
QP259.S39   1988
591.1′6—dc19   87-27475
                                                              CIP

10   9   8   7   6   5

TO
GEORGE BUEHR
(too long gone)
Stand, wherever, take
the bow.

CONTENTS

ACKNOWLEDGMENTS

In the passage thank you.

GUIDING LIGHTS:
Robert Hughes; Michael Denneny; Paul Liepa; John Fleming; Noreen McBride; Claire Henry; Miodrag Mihailovic, M.D.; and André Trent.

GO LIGHTS:
Carol Baldwin; Elizabeth Crown; and Robert H. Resnick.

ILLUMINATIONS:
The Library of Congress; the Newberry Library, Chicago; the New York Public Library; and the Kinsey Institute for Sex Research, Bloomington, Indiana.

STARS:
My family.

PREFACE

The Female Member and how she came is a lickety-split sexual history of the female genital area with a particular focus on that dynamic target—the vagina. This book describes, back to prehistoric times, the female sexual practices of gals having a ball, from many eras and cultures. In a spurt, the reader can also learn the differences and similarities between human and animal sexual behavior. It is a plunging examination of the Why, When, What, and Where of sexual energy from the perspective of the female member.

In a breeze, as the story of the vagina surfaces, the reader will learn the interconnections between current sexual practices and mores and those from ancient cultures. The reader will also learn that there is one vagina in a million—human to boot—capable of conceiving a child without even a tich of sperm; that one, infamous, prostitute retired from her sporty life-style not because she was sixty-five (which she was) but because her son wanted to take her on; that, in the prehistoric Age of Matriarchy, delivery and output of the vagina was deified and the first form of sex worship; that the vagina of the blue whale—the largest on our globe—expands twenty-three feet when, having had a belly full, she delivers her babe; that female "penis envy" is a pipe dream and that the same goes for the frigidity plague that struck vaginas in the nineteenth century; that historically sex ed is a song; that the Vessel is not a pressure cooker when you stir with a divine leakproof tool; and why accounts don't balance in historical vaginal bookkeeping.

And the battle for survival of the fittest is coming to a head in the vaginal chamber for the twenty-first century.

Does this book get to the bottom and deliver the whole story? Hardly, since the vagina, the source for all mankind down through the ages, is fathomless. What this book does do is spread some facts, nail some myths, plug in some dreams, and leak a few secrets.

Kit Schwartz

1

A STAKEOUT OF THE VAGINA

A woman's vagina is located fourteen inches north of her knees, between two legs, hidden behind a bush, under secure cover in a safe house. Because of its low visibility, many speculate about the vagina's clandestine operations as a double agent for input and output. For this investigative report, our code name for vagina is Madame X. And since input is where Madame X does all her maneuvering—output is another book—that's where this surveillance operation will center.

Madame X, even after parting the bush, is a hard one to find. For one thing, she keeps her lips tightly sealed until she is ready to accept an overt operation.

To penetrate her deep cover, one must first crack her security cover. No mean job when one has to measure up to a mount of Venus, the major labia, the minor labia, the hood of a clitoris, a ticklish clitoris, and, on occasion, the feisty hymen. If a probing agent succeeds in penetrating all these security bases, he will, finally, be in a position to attain his desired objective—the blockade of Madame X.

But before you get too cocky, remember, Madame X is out to crease you with the gracious accommodations of her hiding place. If her space is too narrow, don't get into a flap, just get in there, give her a *loving* poke, and she'll expand her walls. Her ceiling too low? She'll raise it to suit your measurement. Her walls too rosy? She'll drape you in purple. Too dry? Madame X, naturally, switches her humidifier on—to *Sweat*.

But watch it—when you start to pump her—she'll make a grab for you. And in an effort to bring you down, after much back and forth, Madame X will discharge you. In the end, you will realize that the grasping Madame X has creamed you once again.

Since she is a deep-cover operator cracked on covert operations, it has been almost impossible (until sex researchers Masters and Johnson zeroed in on the vagina's operating technique during coitus) to get a picture of Madame X when she pulls her shot. Probably the earliest visual was projected in the stone fertility idols carved in cave life around 20,000 B.C. For a vaginal disguise it's a knockout. In those primitive days, Madame X came camouflaged as a faceless, doughy figure clutching—pointedly between generous boobs—a bison's horn. These stony figures were tagged, by some far-sighted art historian, Venus statuettes. Kinda spooky since Venus was not rising to meet the occasion.

Digging really deep, there is a portrait of Madame X in sign language. The vagina camouflaged as a clenched fist with the thumb (surprise! the penis) tucked inside. Then there's that two-faced portrait: Madame X, in deep cover, is a clenched fist, a thumb still tucked inside but now its tip (surprise! the clitoris) pokes out between two middle fingers.

Some art historians claim art originated with erotic cave murals—stone engravings that sensitively portray the human vulva or that of animals, animal animals, doing it.

Speaking of animals—one of the earliest word portraits of the vagina was a zoo-illogical tale that surfaced in India around the fourth century. This zoo story appeared in that jungle of a sex manual entitled the *Kama Sutra*. Here vagina, tagged *yoni* in the East, came camouflaged as an animal. Indeed, as three animals: The Deer (a small vagina); The Mare (a medium-sized vagina); and The Elephant (a colossal bore). Zoo-illogically, the *Kama Sutra* devised a schema enabling males to determine the size of a woman's vagina from her outward appearance and her physical actions. For example, the small vagina, the dear, is possessed by a woman who has a girlish body but solid hips. This Deer would rather do it than eat. Also, she has an active mind and, better yet, a vivid imagination when it comes to doing it. Her yoni juice smells like expensive perfume and her vagina, the dear, does not exceed six finger breadths (in the deer park of five inches).

A vagina in the medium range, designated The Mare, can be spotted on a woman who has "a raised umbilical region." If a male is uncertain about the location of the umbilical region of a Mare, he should look instead for a long neck, a retreating forehead, pretty eyes, and two shapely legs (if your Mare has four, you're being taken for a ride). This Mare is hot to trot and enjoys a good night's sleep. Her yoni juice smells like a lotus flower. If you're concerned this fair one will come to dead halt before you achieve your climax, forget it, you're riding a champion. The Mare does not exceed nine finger breadths (a ravine of seven inches).

The boring colossus, The Elephant, is yawning in

women with short arms but generous boobs. She has a wide face (no mention is made of her ears) and eats like an animal. Her voice rings like a bellow and, hold your nose, her yoni juice smells like an elephant in rut. As would be expected with her gluttonous appetite, she can't get enough of it. The Elephant does not exceed twelve finger breadths (a mammoth of some twelve inches).

One thousand, five hundred and sixty years after this anatomical tale was written, sex therapists Masters and Johnson proved, through probing research, that the average measurement for a woman's vagina (a woman who had borne no more than two children) ranged from seven to eight centimeters in length when not sexually stimulated—a dainty measurement that falls in the category of The Mare. M & J listed no guidelines for determining the size of a woman's vagina from her outward appearance or physical actions. As their research continues to hang in there, the odds seem less than favorable such guidelines ever will.

Elephants—vaginal elephants—must be very big in the East. In medieval times, a Tibetan monk, Padma dkar-po, came up with this description for the vulva: It resembled ". . . the tip of an elephant trunk." God save, this monk did wrap up his description by saying: ". . . and it opens and closes like a lotus flower."

The great explorer Sir Richard Burton dug up some advice for males to spot a woman "cursed" with a large vulva, when he translated an Arabian sheik's sixteenth-century sex manual, *The Perfumed Garden*. Catch this for one royal smear.

> . . . her hair is wooly, her forehead projecting, her eyes are small and blear, her nose is enormous, the lips lead-colored, the mouth large, the cheeks wrinkled and she shows gaps in her teeth; her cheekbones shine purple, and she sports bristles on her chin; her head sits on a meagre neck, with very much developed tendons; her

shoulders are contracted and her chest is narrow, with flabby pendulous breasts, and her belly is like an empty leather-bottle, with the navel standing out like a heap of stones; her flanks are shaped like arcades; the bones on her spinal column may be counted; there is no flesh on her croup; . . . and [she] has large knees and feet like a guitar.

Shaykh Nefzawi, sexist sheik author of *The Perfumed Garden*, has listed thirty-four ungardenlike varieties of vulvas and vaginas, each has a stink all its own:

The Silent One—This name has been given to the vulva that is noiseless. The member may enter it a hundred times a day but will not say a word, and will be content to look on without a murmur.

The Crested One—It is the name given to a vulva furnished with a red comb, like that of a cock, which rises at the moment of enjoyment.

The Swelling One—So called because a torpid member coming near it, and rubbing its head against it a few times, at once swells and stands upright . . . at the moment of crisis it opens and shuts convulsively, like the vulva of a mare.

The Large One—This names applies to the vagina of women who are plump and fat. When such a one crosses her thighs one over the other the vulva stands out like the head of a calf . . . If she lays it bare it resembles corn placed between her thighs; and if she walks, it is apparent under her clothes by its wavy movement at each step.

The Humpbacked—This vulva has the mount of Venus prominent and hard, standing like the hump on the back of a camel, and reaching down between the thighs like the head of a calf.

The Long One—This vulva extends from the pubis to the anus. It lengthens out when a woman is lying down or standing and contracts when she is sitting, differing in this respect from the vulva of a round shape. It looks like a splendid cucumber lying between the thighs.

The sheik goes on, and on, and on and, finally, wraps the vagina in a package he tags "The Sucker." Since it is not for adult reading, we'll blow it and wind up with this poetry from anonymous—the sheik had sense enough to wish the poet "may God grant all his wishes in Paradise!"

Anonymous paints a fairer portrait—other than the pipe dream he paints on the length of a male's pecker—for the vulva and the vagina:

> Like a man extended on his chest, [ah-men, that
> is one inflated figure!] she—the vulva—fills the
> hand. Which has to be well stretched out to cover
> it. The place it occupies is standing forth
> Like an unopened bud of the blossom of a palm tree.
> Assuredly the smoothness of its skin
> Is like the beardless cheek of adolescence;
> Its conduit is but narrow,
> The entrance to it is not easy,
> And he who essays to get in
> Feels as though he were butting against a coat of mail.
> And at the introduction it emits a sound
> Like to the tearing of a woven stuff.
> The member having filled its cavity,
> Receives the lively welcome of a bite,
> . . . Its lips are burning,
> Like a fire that is lighted,
> And how sweet it is, this fire! . . .

In the West, descriptions of the vagina and vulva were no-no's in poetry, literature, religion, books, indeed, everywhere but medical books—and those were printed in Latin for the public good. So over centuries, the public came up with a list of euphemisms and synonyms to describe what the hell it is that had everyone tongue-tied.

As you wade through this gassy swamp, it will cheer your heart if you keep in mind: A hotshot operator such as Madame X survives, indeed thrives, on the screw up in compartmentalization.

EUPHEMISMS AND SYNONYMS FOR FEMALE GENITALS IN THE WESTERN WORLD

At Bay for Pigs
Yum-yum
Sampler
Orange
Number nip
Fig
Eel skin
Bum shop
Cornucopia
Melting pot
Spermsucker
Apricot split
Supper
Meat cooker
Coffee house
Jelly bag
The icing
Crumpet
Hairburger
Hairpie
Gape
Bun
Dumb glutton
Bottomless pit

At Bay for Pigs (cont.)
Sugar donut
Yeast-powder biscuit
Lobster-pot
Mutton
Jelly-roll
Jam-pot
Bit of jam
Jelly
Cake
Butter boat
Cookie
Meat
Cream jug
Sugar basin
Honey pot
Milk jug
Mustard pot
Oyster
Pancake
Oat bin
Golden donut
Muffin
Bread

At Bay for Pigs (cont.)
Free fishery
Hot beef
Gravy maker
Green grocery
Bit on a fork
Fleshy part

Overload
Twitcher
Hey nonny nonny and a
  hot cha-cha
Squint
Bawdy monosyllable
Dicky-Dido
Fanny-Artful
A belly dingle
Funniment
Diddle
Funny bit
Toyshop
Diddle case
Flapdoodle
Coozie
Black joke
Whim wham
Under dimple
Fiddle

No-knock Entry
Grandmother's house
Home sweet home
Little sister
Sharp and blunt
Buttonhole worker

No-knock Entry (cont.)
Valley of Decision
The grindstone
Crack
Bread winner
Name it not
Little Miss Cradle

Sanitized
The Gym
Football field
Sportsman's hole
Pit pitcher
Front gut
Jock
Fly catcher
A sport
Divine scar
Bob and hit
Aphrodisical tennis court
Gymnasium

Ad Hoccery
ABC
Whatsis
Affair
Certificate of birth
Front Office
She
Whoosis
Thingumabob
Thingamagig
Center of attraction
Sex
Whaddya call it

Liquidity
Halfpenny
Gate of plenty
Hog eye
Spender
Budget
House of security
Creased
In a flap
Poor man's blessing
Solution of continuity
Pleasure house

Flap Potential
Mantrap
Prick-pocket
Snatch-blatch
Naughty
The hot box
Fie-for-shame
Gaper
Rob-the-Ruffian
Snatch
Eye that weeps
Down the hatch
Pisser
Carnal trap
Rough and tumble
Snatch box
Snippet
Square push
The satchel
The case
The never out trap
Fornicator's hall

Flap Potential (cont.)
Pleasure house
Gig

Cock Phooey
Cockpit
Cock Alley
Cock Inn
Cock loft
Cockshire
Cock holder
Cock Lane
Cock Hall
Cock
Cockshy
Rooster

Close Up Shop!
Rest and be thankful
Four-letter word
Buckinger's boot
Fart-Daniel
Bluebeard's closet
Gutter
Fool-trap
Bile
Brat-getting
Fly-trap
Wound
Skin the pizzle
Target
Pit-hole
Poxbox
Prick scourer
Rough and tumble

9

Close Up Shop! (cont.)

Privy Hole
Ass
Mark of the beast
Peculiar river
Slit
Crinkum-crankum
Baby-maker
Chuff box
Cat's meat
Coolie-do
Doodle-sack
Cuckoo's nest
Itching Jenny
Hone
Dumb-squint
Eye that weeps most when best pleased
Sear
Belly entrance
Undertaker
Slot
Bum fiddle
Bull's eye
Nick-in-the-notch
Main vein
Shaft companion

Entitlement

A jewel
Center of bliss
A universe
Fountain of life
Irish fortune
Lady Jane

Entitlement (cont.)

Lady Berkeley
Lady Star
Lady Flower
The Forecastle
Marble arch
The treasury
An ornament
The exchequer
Scabbard
Nature's tufted treasure
Jack Straw's castle
Queen of holes
Fortress

Deep Six!

The channel
Pleasure-boat
Harbor of Hope
Cape of Good Hope
Forehatch
Hatchway
Botany Bay
Port-hole
Notch
Love's channel
Love's harbour
Leak
Little man in the boat
Boy in the boat
Cape Horn
Scuttle
Sally Port
Half Moon Bay
Mate

Deep Six! (cont.)
Oyster catcher
Cunt

On-High Profile
Heavenly part
Holy of Holies
Mother of all masons
Divine monosyllable
Generating place
Mother of all saints
Mother of all souls
Mouth that can not bite
Seminary
Glory hole

A Credibility Gap
That
What
Bore
Stuff
Machine
Parenthesis
Monosyllable
Factotum
You know what

Office for Strategic Service
Altar of hymen
Paradise
Venus's honeypot
Portal of Venus
Road to heaven
Venus's cell

Office for Strategic Service (cont.)
Temple of low men
Temple of Venus

Stonewalling
Hymen
Virginale
Virgin's head
Claustrom virginale
Maidenhead
Maid's ring
Virgin knot
Membrum mulibers
Maiden gear
Modesty

Up Front
Forecaster
Forewoman
Fore-room
Forecastle
Fore-court
Front piece
Upright grin
Upright wink

Cosmetizing
Button
Muff
Purse
Placket hole
Leather
Milliner's shop
Old hat
Slipper

Cosmetizing (cont.)

Hoop
Fan
Bag
Beauty spot
Fur
Trinket
Lower wig
Pocket book
Skin coat
Sweet scented hole
Sheath
Trinket
Beaver
Hairy ring
Unders
Under dimple
Carvel's ring
Bearded lady
Black velvet

Needs Laundering

Dirty barrel
Dog's mouth
Suck and swallow
Chat
Gasp and grunt
Mouth thankless
Growl
Hairy oracle
Moose
Naggie
Old thing
Old woman
Old ding
Old wife

The Alien

Penis
Penis equivalent
Penis muliebris

Deep Cover

Pussy
Cat's meow
Cat's-head-cut-open
Bee-hive
Squirrel
Mouse
Mouser
Mouse-trap
Catch-'em-alive-o
Cloven tuft
Cat's meat
Horse collar
Civet
Hogstyle of Venus
Shell
Poontang
Chicken's tongue

Devised Facility

Field for ploughing
Pumpkin
Red onion
Fish pond
Cabbage
Cherry
Cauliflower
Water-mill
Patch
Old Mossyface
Periwinkle

Garden of Eden

Thatch

Fruitful vine

Central furrow

Front garden

Daisy

Green meadow

Intercrural trench

Grotto

Black-hole

Ace at spades

Flower of chivalry

Seed-land

Seed-plot

Orchard

Rose

Happy Valley

Grove of Eglantine

Pleasure garden

Belly-dale

Hive

Gulley-hole

Furrow

Ivory gate

Bird

Goldfinch's nest

Dilbery-bush

Cabbage-patch

Fountain of love

Bush

Bushy-park

Tit mouse

Flower heart

Upper Holloway

Covered way

Wayside fountain

Bower of bliss

Grass

Bog

Gentlemen's pleasure garden

Gray Area

Hairyfordshire

Gyvel

Bombo

Claff

Kaze

Gallimaufrey

Futy

Futz

Cooch

Contrapunctum

Pudenda

Pudenda muliebris

Pudendum

Medlar

Mons meg

Mons pubis

Mons veneris

Quem

Quiff

Quimmy

Quin

Scut

Rough malkin

Almanach

Bazoo

Charley Hunt

Buckfinger's boot

Keifer

Conundrum
Ineffable
Hypogastric-cranny
Cunnikin
Firelock
Chocha
Boody
Jiggumbob
Twin
Twatchel
Quoniam
Rattle ballocks
Ringerrangerroo
Teazle
The Antipodes
Tench
Whelk
Twittle
Tive
Tu quroque
Twat
Cony
Theca
Claff
Coot
Fobus
Vulva
Vagina
Clitoris
Female
Pudend
C.
O.B.H
Long-eye

Cogie
Nonesuch

Special Operations

Box
Chimney
Clock
Knick-knack
Ladder
Corner
Alcove
Bungalow
Coffee-grinder
Cellar-door
Churn
Keyhole
Gravy giver
Cellar
Front porch
Front window
Front parlor
Front door
Front attic
Broom
Fireplace
Handle for the broom
Drain
Pot
Butcher shop
Thatched house
Yard measure
Milking pail
Mortar
Sluice

14

Special Operations (cont.)

Tool chest
Valve
Lather maker
Vacuum
Middle gate
Pin-case
Receiving set
Match
Meat cooker
Locker
Milk pan
Needle book
Niche
Lock
Meat grinder
Shake bag
Ware
Water box
Socket
Leading article
Chink
Love chamber
Nick-nack
Plaything
Pipe cleaner
Vent
Rasp
Bell
Cup
Waste pipe
Salt cellar
Candlestick
Regulator
Workshop

Special Operations (cont.)

Button factory
Oven
Kitchen
Corner cupboard
Downstairs
Furnace
Nook
Pan

Clandestine Operation

Downtown
Lapland
Postern gate to the Elysian
 Field
Cupid's Alley
Burial ground
Fuck hole
Gap
Geography
Gate of life
Lowlands
Netherlands
Under the hill
Quarry
Circle
Keystone of love
Ingle-nook
India
China
Dead end street
Gulley hole
South Pole
Tunnel
Miraculous cairn

Clandestine Operation (cont.)

Middle Kingdom
Puddle
Spew Alley
Love Lane
Low country
Midlands
Spot
Nether end
Manhole
Lapland
Trench
Private parts
Playground
Where Uncle Diddle goes
Cave of Harmony
Chink
Love's paradise
Smock Alley
Shady Spring
Limbo
Spot
Matrix
Main Street
Love's pavilion
Mill
Road
Gateway
Stream Town

Contingency Funding

Fort Knox
Money Box
Toll Box
Receipt of custom

Contingency Funding (cont.)

Mine of pleasure
Spender
Milker
Hole of holes
Commodity
Eve's custom house
Hole of Content
A gusher
The bank
The business
Concern
The till
Jewel enclosure
The vault

Moles

Fanny-fair
Brown Miss
Cleft of flesh
Gigi
Bunny
Womanhood
Star
Madge
Kitty
Dimples
Crown and feathers
Bimbo
Girl Street
Pretty
Miss Laycock
Mary Jane
Flusey
Tirly-whirly

Moles (cont.)
Black Bess
Tootsie wootsie

Double Agents
Tomboy
Adam's own
Roasting Jack
Chum
Toby
Charley
Joe Hunt
Black Jack
Mickey Mouse
Gray Jock

A Task with Force
The Saddle
Berkshire hunt
Sportsman's gap
Go down to the finish line

The Oval Office
Crotch
Ace
Gut entrance
Spitfire
Wham
Box unseen
Pandora's box

The Plumbers
Tail
Tail feathers
Tail gate
Tail box
Tail hole
Tail gap
Tail trimmer
Tail end
The end

But, is that the end? The above list includes nearly 640 nicknames for the female genitals—twice as many as those recorded for the male—but then, a female's genitals have more moving parts.

In the late nineteenth century, one record totaled up 650 alternate usages for the "filthy" term *cunt*. Cunt has needed all the aliases it could gather, since it was banned from print in Britain from 1300 to the middle of the twentieth century. Even today cunt is considered the most undesirable word in the English language. For the delight of playing naughty, here are cunt's dearest nicknames: cunniken, cuntlet, cunny, cuntkin, and cunnicle.

The origin of the term *cunt* remains a mystery to this day.

The Encyclopedia of Sexual Behavior suggests the presence of the plosive "k" in certain sexual terms in use in the English language could be equated with the vocalized dynamics of intercourse. It was the ancient Romans, via Latin, who tuned the Western world's ear into the elegant—but macho—sound of vagina, meaning sheath. The sheath protects a sword from rusting or dust. Pointless to add, Latin for penis is sword.

The Oxford English Dictionary (1981) defines vagina as "The membranous canal leading from the vulva to the uterus in women and female animals . . . A part or formation serving as or suggestive of a sheath; a sheath like covering, organ or part; a theca [a sac]."

When Madame X, and her security blanket, opt for a romantic disguise, she shops in the East. As opposed to in the West, there she can wrap herself in the plumes of Mother Nature or the jewels worthy of a queen.

In the Field
Conch shell
Anemone of love
Wheat Shaped cave
Heart of the peony
Inner stream
Sexual cavern
Love grotto
Inner heart
Mysterious valley
Perfumed mouse
Pleasure grotto
Lotus flower
Pleasure field of heaven
Lotus of her wisdom
Inner terrace
Sensitive cave
Seat of wisdom

The Deer
The Mare
(Let us stand tall and overlook The Elephant).

A Sphere of Influence
Red pearl
Treasure house
Jade gate
Jeweled enclosure
Precious stone
Golden doorway
Door of life
Female crucible
Pleasure palace
Strings of the lyre
Precious crucible

In the West, after the 1950s, medical science decided to make an exploratory search for the "true" Madame X. And to date, no one has made a more in depth study of the inner operation of Madame X's decompression chamber than Masters and Johnson.

Scientists that they are, these two researchers prefer using the code name of "vaginal barrel" for Madame X. First they discovered that as tensions (sexual) rise, Madame X—oops! vaginal barrel—begins to sweat. Then, "as tensions increase, the droplets coalesce to form a smooth, glistening coating for the entire barrel." In other words, Madame X is prepared for action. In action, "Initially, there is a lengthening and distension of the inner two-thirds of the vaginal barrel." Before Madame X's excitement peaks, this expansion goes from 2 cm up to a range of 5.75 to 6.25 cm from the neck up. From the nape of her neck to the top of the head, Madame X stretches from 7 to 8 cm to 9.5 to 10.5 cm. Also Madame X's puss turns from a purplish-red to a dark purple (well, what did they expect—that's a lot of blowing up to do all on your lonesome, especially when you're under the gun of survival of the fittest).

After the vaginal barrel shapes up and excitement continues to mount, Masters and Johnson observed, "this localized area of bulbar vasoconcentration contracts strongly in a regularly recurring pattern during the orgasmic expression." In other words, Madame X is shaking down her ammunition. The lady is about to explode. And the beauty of Madame X is that the lady has more ammunition then she knows what to do with. After she wipes out an intruder, she is capable of putting on, not just one, but countless numbers of her explosive routines.

In all of nature, Madame X is unique. In fact, indeed, she is much more than one dynamite dame.

2

LIGHT AT THE END OF A TUNNEL

"Man—a creature made at the end of the week's work when God was tired."

—Mark Twain

But then God, after a sensible rest, made Eve. And, inside of Eve, God tucked the first vagina. Or so, in essence, the Good Book says.

For a different tale tune in biology.

Biologists claim the vagina, or a primitive pattern for it, took its sweet time, over 100 million years, before it semisurfaced on this globe. When it finally made the plunge, the vagina evolved in a primitive group of reptiles called the sauria, better known as dinosaurs, lizards, crocodiles, and tortoises. Note: This tale is a far piece from the

Garden of Eden, since even the snake is excluded. Female snakes do not, biowise, have vaginas (although male snakes have a crude prototype of a penis). Snakes Do It via the anus (the cloaca) as do most amphibians, birds, and many fish.

The cloaca, a zoologist's term for a sewer, was/is nature's primitive pattern for the vagina (and the penis, too, after nature came up with the trick of the snake protruding its anus). Cloacas work best for those who have no need to stand on their feet the better part of a day.

Still, whether cloaca or vagina, locating the female member is beyond the depth of many. To get over that hump and into the groove, let's poke around for a few.

One female in nature lets it all hang out *if* she pulls her head in. When her season is ripe for mating, the female land tortoise gains so much weight that if she pulls her head inside of her crusty shell, her cloaca/vagina pops out her rear.

The female cardinal fish is no lady. First, this fishy lady has a cloaca she can enlarge when *she* decides to mate and, second, she uses this firm tool to plunge inside—and up—the male's anus.

The female snail has her vagina in her head. Another heady one is the female octopus, who has her vagina in her nose—or what should pass for one, since she uses the same tube for breathing. The stuffy male octopus has found this vagina/nose nothing to sneeze at. The female octopus is not always in the mood, so when a male pokes her in the nose with one of his eight arms that acts as a penis, this feisty dame has been known to bite off his penis/arm and swim away with it. This is one snotty lady the male would have been wise to snub.

Everyone detests bedbugs but the male bedbug is the most detestable. This creep has such a warped penis, it can't reach her vagina, so instead he stabs the lady in the back with his twisted pecker. Even though the blood she sheds, after a human attack, might be yours, salute the ladybug. No one deserves to get It in the back.

The most unreal vagina of all is a cannibal, and the most unreal thing about this vagina, which is tucked inside a bumblebee eelworm, is that it absorbs, gradually, the body surrounding it. In *How They Do It*, Robert Wallace claims this lady-killer vagina becomes "a giant organ about twenty thousand times as large" as the female body it has absorbed. To locate this gobbling genital, look for a hibernating bumblebee who has just about had It, for this worm then uses the body tissue of the bee as a nest—and food—till she gives birth to more lady-killer vaginas. As might be predicted, the male eelworm curled up and died after introducing his pecker to this devastating vagina.

The vagina of the termite is another example of a gainfully employed female organ. The queen of a termite colony—the only female with a functioning vagina—produces 132 million baby termites in her twelve-year reign. Having babes increases the size of most vaginas, so you may well imagine what queenie's vagina expands to after a few years of such intensive breeding. Rex Freedman in *Sex Link* says the queen's body turns into a reproduction factory with an assembly line working overtime. In order to impregnate her, the king, who has the sole pecker in the colony, "must squirm and slide and push his way under her gross sausage like body before he can reach her genitals and copulate with her."

The blue whale has the most expansive vagina on our globe. After accommodating the ten-foot penis of the male, she, true blue, when *her* time comes, lengthens the vaginal passage to deliver a twenty-three foot bambino.

The butterfly, that changeling, has two vaginas—one for input, one for output.

Some vaginas, like that of the female bumblebee eelworm's, are killers. The most deadly of all kill by gobbling the pecker that penetrates them. The vagina of the queen bee gets a choke hold on the pecker of the drone *after* he ejaculates. When he tries to fly away, the queen's vagina disembowels the drone, who, in a state of shocking deflation, goes into a deadly tailspin. When the drone hits terra firma, he is DOA.

Praying has never saved the male mantis. Not only does he lose his pecker and bod, he's doomed to Do It dead. But Ms. mantis knows there's life in the old boy yet, for this killer has discovered if she bites off his head, that after passing on, his pecker becomes alive-a-live-oh. And the more of his body she gobbles, the more orgasmic becomes the male's organ in her vagina. After her mouth gobbles him from head to toe, her vagina proceeds to chew up his pecker. Or so we must assume, for Ms. Mantis' vagina has never been known to belch out a pecker.

Another gobbler is the female scorpion. Once her vagina has been satisfied, this lady killer, who is capable of not eating for an entire year, makes a meal of her mate—pecker, et cetera.

The most infamous lady killer after Doing It is that charmer, the female black widow spider. Males in this species are never referred to as black widowers, since they seldom get the opportunity to bury a mate. The female—six times his size—usually does the courting, and once she has succeeded engaging his tiny pecker (which she probably has never forgiven him for), she then makes a grab for the rest of him. If he is fast on his eight tiny feet, madam has to wait for another entanglement to become a full-fledged widow.

If you spot a sea horse dragging his tail, you may be assured it's the undone male. For, not only is he one of the few males whose pecker has been replaced by a vagina (or the equivalent of one), he is the only male to carry the burden of pregnancy. There is small evidence the male sea horse enjoys the switch Mother Nature—pulling a double switch—yanked off him when she gave the female of his species what was "rightfully" his. Even in courtship, the male sea horse's penis envy is evident, for he makes no approach to court the well-endowed female when she slithers up to him flashing her tail. Resigned to his fate, he tucks his head to one side as he submits to the "lady's" embrace, when her so-called pecker pops a packet in his pocket. Flashing her tail, she scoots away for a life of play. After these encounters, the male sea horse has been known to brood, a lot.

There is one vagina, in the lizard world, that has no interest in a male's pecker. And it best not, since none exist, not even in reproduction. In the United States and parts of Mexico, this all-female species is known as the whiptailed lizard. And while these Amazons seem a little frantic as they race around whipping their tails, no evidence has surfaced that this species suffers from the lack of a pecker.

But the whiptailed lizard isn't the only one capable of reproducing on its own. There is one rare species of human vagina that mimics the Do-It-yourself skill of this lizard. This vagina, according to Helen Spurway, a British eugenic specialist, appears in 1.6 million pregnancies. It also gives a scientific boost to the "case" supporting the nonsexual reproduction capability of the Virgin Mary.

Throughout most of documented time, a female somewhere in the world has declared she has conceived without the "benefit" of sexual relations. And everyone sniggered, especially the medical profession—until 1955, when a group of English scientists decided to investigate the claim of Miss Emmie Marie Jones. In 1944, during a bombardment in Hanover, Germany, Ms. Jones collapsed from possible shock and extreme exhaustion. Nine months later, Ms. Jones gave birth to a daughter, which was an even bigger shock to her than the Allies' bombs, since she—with ever-growing persistence—claimed to be a virgin. As the years passed, Ms. Jones and her daughter, with the exception of age difference, looked—and acted—like identical twins.

When the British scientists concluded their tests, they

could only back up Ms. Jones' virgin birth claim, since they found no difference in genetic makeup between the mother and the daughter.

Later, at a meeting of the American Neurological Association, a Dr. Walter Timme reported an even stranger case. After removing an ovarian tumor from a sixteen-year-old girl, also a virgin, a pathologist report documented finding live eggs *and* live sperm in the tumor. Dr. Timme is quoted as saying this was "a true case of where the physical setup was possible for a virgin birth."

Currently, human nonsexual conception is getting it piecemeal from both barrels in several areas of the world. But, when it comes down to Doing It for the fun of It, the vagina still works up a sweat—*after* a modicum of sweat-shopping.

3

SWEAT-SHOPPING

Prostitutes, working out by the hour, have no time for foreplay. To prosper, these pros have trained their bodies to turn on the vaginal sweat as soon as some jock hits their wall. But for most females—including pros when they're not working out—breaking the vagina into an invitational sweat requires getting psyched up—which, for the majority, means courtship. Courtship takes many forms. And it isn't only the human gal who requires a certain amount of sweat-shopping before buying It.

For centuries, the human animal believed that all other animals did it like clockwork. Seasonal alarm clocks rang, and bang, they—those animals!—were banging away. This cock and bull is a fishy tale that made the rounds until Darwin dropped his ancestral bomb. It was then that man decided to take a deeper look into his animal heritage, dumb as it was. After lengthy investigation, man discovered, with sullen amazement, that many species in the nonhuman world were capable of strategic thought and action when it came right down to getting something they wanted or needed.

And, after all these years, man continues to be amazed he isn't the only living thing on this globe with some horse sense. Take a 1984 news report that relates how astonished a naturalist was when he discovered, after two years of observation, that lions in Africa were intelligent enough not only to plan a battle strategy, but to synchronize it and time a conquest to a T. Bug-eyed, the naturalist observed a pride of lions, all females—even more astounding—crawl, one by one, on their bellies in high grass until they had their target, a group of zebras, surrounded. The pride, all ten, left one area of their circle unguarded, where the wind, in a sudden gust, would blow in toward their target. The lions lay, independently, crouched for over an hour, waiting without tipping a twitch. Finally, in a strategic moment, when the wind picked up, one female lion appeared and charged down the unguarded stretch toward the prey. Catching this lion's scent, the zebras made a run for it—right into the waiting jaws of the other crouched lions.

The astounded scientist rattled on about the high level of intelligence it took to plot this intricate waiting game—a strategy of teamwork so complex it equaled, in many areas, the superior intelligence of man.

This covert, and overt, operation zeroed in on filling their bellies with food. The naturalist—and others—should keep the other eye peeled on how all dumb animals plot when it comes to yet another form of survival—reproduction of their species. For this operation, many a breed uses a combination of penetrating analysis, sabotage, propaganda, and counterespionage—a scam so sophisticated it would put many a devious human to shame.

Take that angler—the male ceratoid fish. In the spooky darkness of the deep sea, he searches not only for a mate but a lifetime meal ticket. This slug is a total parasite. He spies out an unsuspecting mate, delivers a single biting kiss—preferably on her food-smacking lips—and then never, ever lets go. His body, which sucks, becomes one with the female's lips and tongue. *The New Larousse Encyclopedia* reports, "Nearly all the organs of the dwarf male degenerate, except [ah yes, old blood and guts] the reproductive one." Once smacked, for the rest of her days, the female has to swim drooling a male organ. Does her fat lip put this gal in a shocking state? On the contrary, this angler must have enjoyed getting smacked, since she swims around, drooling the male organ, advertising what a great provider she could be. Her direct-male campaign must succeed, for many a female angler is swimming around—merci, in the dark—dangling male organs after being smacked by suckers again and again.

Grabbing a sneaky kiss or an embrace is a courting method used by many species in the nonhuman world and, although some are more tender than others, almost all are rodlike cohesive. There is Hairy the Frog, who grows hair on his flanks only during the breeding season in order to cushion the shock of his rear embrace as he pins, with a croak, his pop-eyed mate. Yet another species of male frog grabs so hard—and so often—he develops unfeeling calluses on his fingers and forearms (which some human "animal" has tagged "nuptial pads").

Males don't take all the honors when it comes to grabbing off a mate. Take those warrior female lions who for hours stalked their unsuspecting prey for a timely slaughter; one can't imagine those aggressive cats letting any male off a hook if they decide that's the chunk they want to mate. And sprightly so, since a pride of lions averages out to eleven go-get-him females and one bushed male. Beggars don't get chosen with this unbalanced ratio, so the female usually takes the aggressive initiative when it comes to courting. What's a shocker is her attention-grabbing method—a swift, hard slap across his man-eating jaws, because the svelte lioness is no match for the male in size (who weighs in at 500 pounds and, without a stretch, is 10 feet in length, not including his snappy tail).

When she is not in heat, a lioness yawns a lot, especially when Leo is around. Small wonder, since this king of the beasts is also reputed to be the laziest male in the jungle. The lioness takes full charge when it comes to raising her cubs. They never leave her protective care until they are ready to tear a piece of the jungle apart. This hefty care requires tons of food, and female lions do 90 percent of the hunting in a pride. As for Leo, he works at roaring and pissing—scare tactics for warning off nomad males from moving in on *his* pride.

But, when it comes down to doing it, Leo proves indeed that he is king. After the female slaps down her initial invitation, the male lion is capable of scoring for three days—and nights—straight, every *fifteen minutes*. Small wonder Leo's life is one big yawn till next heat season pops him up.

Cornered in captivity, lions of either sex are not choosy. This cat will mate with other breeds of the big cat family. These hybrid species have hybrid names; that is, an offspring of a lioness and a tiger is a tigon; an offspring of a lioness and a leopard is leopon. No mention is made of a lioness mating with a jaguar, but the end result could be called a jagon.

Syncopated rituals in mating are not uncommon in the wild. For some species of birds and snakes, it's a shake till they break marathon. Their choreography is limited but their stamina is admirable. The spindle legs of some male birds know not from stop as they tap a solo for hours till a mate decides it's time for two to tango. Snakes in some species choose a dancing partner and shake, from torso, neck, and head, till one—usually the male—drops in a hypnotic swoon, signaling love me and leave me; you are too much.

The male lizard, a creep and a sneak, uses the female's less-armored throat for a choke hold while his hind limbs lock her to the crush of submission as one of his two penes take turns ramming her cloaca. The male lizard is also into homosexuality and is an endless terror, for when not making it, he is apt to chomp off another's tail, gobble it down, and leave him minus a whip and defenseless.

B.O. and sappy secretions are other turn-ons in jungle-style mating. Take the male crocodile, who wafts a scent we term musk. His musk is a must to turn around the snappy temper of a jawsome female croc.

When Dumbo is up for a hump, he gets drippy, secreting *his* sex signal called musth. It is a heavy, brown gook that leaks from glands located behind Dumbo's giant-size, fan-shaped ears. Fanning his stinky musth in the female's direction is not the turn on for the female elephant. Instead, what is the must for the female when she's hot for a hump, is the male's stinking (to high heaven) penis in erection. In a breeze—this stink that carries as far as forty elephant paces—it's no wonder females refuse to associate with the males unless they're in heat, for, with her long, sensitive nose, one whiff could knock this snooty dame over on a heatless day.

Sexually the heat season doesn't exist for the human female. And according to some males, in particular cultures, the female is never capable of getting heated up for Doing It because, poor thing, she is physically frigid. (A meltdown on the snow job called frigidity will come later. For now let's soak in the sweat of this tropic zone.)

Until the second half of the twentieth century, many males, and *many* a female, had to listen to a half-assed tale when it came to the true history of female sexuality (physically).

The true bloom of female sexuality was unearthed in 1953 in Bloomington, Indiana, when Alfred C. Kinsey published the results of interviews conducted with 5,940 females in *Sexual Behavior of the Human Female*. Kinsey's a pet for his data. Although primarily based on human female statistics, it also includes the mating habits of females in the animal world. He also calls turn-ons for the human vagina, "petting." It's an outmoded term for our outspoken age, so let's examine Kinsey's definition for petting: "Physical contacts between females and males which do not involve a union of the genitalia. . . . The term petting is properly confined to physical contacts which involve a deliberate attempt to effect erotic arousal."

Techniques for petting were broken down under these breakthroughs: simple kissing, deep kissing, breast stimulation, mouth-breast contacts, manual stimulation of female genitalia, manual stimulation of male genitalia, oral contact with female genitalia, and oral contact with male genitalia.

But, in a crotchshell, Kinsey found that most females enjoyed, participated in, and looked forward to the continuum of petting. And, as might be anticipated, for those gals who continued on to coitus, the majority umpty-humped even higher.

Another quaint statistic: Kinsey found there was a dramatic breakdown for those gals born on or after 1910. Take this sole statistic for females who got in sweat from deep kissing: Forty-four percent of the gals born before 1900 dug it, as opposed to 74 percent who were born in 1910 or later. This could be proof that there is nothing like a war to loosen up the morals and jack up the morale. Or rather, there's nothing like a war, which gives a woman a job and a decent wage to fight her own battle for financial and sexual independence.

And still another:

Deep kissing, mouth-breast, and mouth-genital contacts were the most taboo of the petting techniques among older generations. Such taboos were sometimes rationalized on hygienic bases. The younger generation [1910 on], ignoring the theoretic hygiene, more often accepts oral techniques—without any dire effects on their health.

Oh, Alfred, you are one for the books!

For a more contemporary perspective of sweatshopping, let's squeeze out some of the statistics that turned up in a study of female sexuality made by *Cosmopolitan* magazine *(The Cosmo Report)* in 1981. This study came up with a total of 106,000 women interviewed. A total that swamped every previous study made on almost anything, and everything.

Zero in on these responses to the query "What do you find pleasant accompaniments or preliminaries to sex?" Topping the list, 7,722 preferred—now Hear This!—the sound of music; 6,480 toasted for a drink (or three); 5,632 snot noses opted for smell (perfume, body odor, etc.); 4,805 flapped for sexy talk; 2,912 got turned on by drugs (pot, "uppers," etc.); pornography peaked 2,121; 1,680 gobblers went down for food; and 780 sneaks replied "other."

What about "that time of the month"? Kinsey found that close to 90 percent of the women interviewed preferred having sex during the premenstrual phase. And Masters and Johnson, in later research, found that females produce more lubrication during this phase. Both data give mounting support that the human gal, while not in heat, has her individual sweat season.

What peaks gals, in any season, is up for grabs. Proof: Of

the gals responding to a Cosmo query "What areas, other than the clitoris, respond erotically to stimulation?" 8,730 swelled for breasts or nipples; 6,461 had a crush on the mouth; 5,670 were grabbed by the ears; 2,651 were stuck-up about the anus; 2,518 *real* sneaks replied "other"; and 81 shrugged "none." As for heavy sweatshopping, nothing can top the clitoris for female genital stimulation. Kinsey, alone, proves that with a statistical report on tests made on 879 gals for sensitivity of the clitoris and other parts of the genitalia. Two percent seemed unaware of tactile stimulation, while 98 percent were *more* than aware. For Kinsey says, "there is considerable evidence that most women respond erotically, often with considerable intensity and immediacy, whenever the clitoris is tactilely stimulated."

When it gets down to splitting hairs, the clitoris is unique. For once it has been activated, it gets so beefed up it could blow you away. It's also out of sight, a hardhead with stick-to-itiveness, never out of bloody circulation after a climax, to the king's taste, to the queen's taste, plus a unique entity in that it has no other function than to initiate and elevate levels of dynamic sexual tension. With all that going for it, no wonder the clitoris gets a swollen head.

Still, before it gets activated, it's so tiny that drawing a bead on the clitoris isn't always easy. For most it's the size a petit pois (pea)—although there are, though rare, some the size of a green bean. And, happy as a clam, the clitoris lies protected beneath a major labia, a minor labia, and a clitoral hood. But when it's out for a blast, the clitoris retracts these protective coverings and bursts, after ground swell, into one dynamite of a bloom.

But first we have to find the little darling. In her book *Woman to Woman*, gynecologist Lucienne Lanson gives us some pointers on how to locate this strategic area. She advises a gal to go on this treasure hunt with a hand mirror for:

Although most of the clitoris is actually hidden from view beneath muscle and fibrous tissue, its tip or glans can be seen as a small pink fleshy projection (about the size of an eraser on the end of a lead pencil). You still can't find the clitoris? Hmm. Press gently where you think the clitoris might be and you will notice a pleasant sensation. Continue to gently prod this area and you may experience a mounting excitement. That is the clitoris.

When a gal physically stimulates her clitoris, it is a very private love affair. And the manipulation of psychoscientific theories—that, subconsciously, her clitoris is a substitute for the penis—brings a rub against her grain. As a penile pecking order, this theory popped up in the early twentieth century when Sigmund Freud opened his canful of beans. Freud's sexist theory claimed little girls, as bare tots in a comparison study, were fated to make a "momentous discovery"—one of towering influence—the penis. Extended to full height, even in a state of collapse, his monument was so superior in size to her own small organ that "from this time forward [she] fell a victim to envy for the penis." From this envy developed an idea that she was castrated. Wounded to her core, she then develops a sense of basic inferiority. Does this little green-eyed monster stop there? Nope. She's out, private eyeing, to detect whether other girls are peckerless like she. Spying nary a female pecker, this little poop develops contempt for her entire sex—starting, naturally, with Mommy dearest. As to making an in-depth investigation of her own vagina, this shortchanged, shortsighted, green-eyed private dick is cross-eyed, busy spying on male crotches.

Freud, impotent most of his life, used scientific logic to lay on his penis theory. But, given a proper grip on it—exploration of the dynamic clitoris—he might with logic have analyzed: Why, ever, would a gal trade her atomic bomb for some guy's cannon?

Now, here's a tip for those males in the fog of ignorance, trying to beat through the brush to get a handle on the tiny clitoris: Stop looking for that "little man in the boat." He's a mirage, a pipe dream, sighted back in the eighteenth century by some English navvy caught in his macho fog. And, if fishing for some inner clue from out of the past, don't pull up anchor when you find that the etymologists' source for clitoris translates "shut up." It comes down from ancient Greece, and we know what they were into, right?

Or those early-twentieth-century embryologists who, leaning backward, fell into a penile trap as they drew a bead on the clitoris in their discovery and research of the human embryo. Their sightings confirmed that until the third month, the human embryo was asexual. It was, then, like a butterfly emerging out of its cocoon; the penis burst upon the embryo's scene and developed rapidly to prove indeed it was a full-grown prick. But what of the embryo that had a start of a penis but, try as it should, didn't pull through and make it to becoming an all-around prick? Ah, that tiny dwarf—the clitoris—just didn't have the necessary guts (you know, testes) to pull it off. And that, pal, is how embryologists determined the clitoris was a retarded penis. Talk about the mirage of "little man in the boat!"

In 1966, at last, at last, researchers Masters and Johnson pulled the plug to sink that "little man" and hoist their mainsail that identified the clitoris as the forceful thrust for a dreamboat. For Masters and Johnson in their log said:

> The clitoris is a unique organ in the total of human anatomy. Its express purpose is to serve as a receptor and transformer of sensual stimuli. Thus, the human female has an organ system which is totally limited in physiologic function to initiating or elevating levels of sexual tension. No such organ exists within the anatomic structure of the human male.

35

The clitoris charts its own course, since, with the pitch of fore and aft, once out of dry dock, the clitoris is up and on *its* way. With wind in its sail, it's full steam ahead.

Masters and Johnson also give a tip for those males who are aloft, and in search of a clitoris on a broad reach:

> Most marriage manuals advocate the technique of find-
> ing the clitoris and remaining in direct contact with it
> during attempts to stimulate female sexual tensions. In
> direct manipulation of the clitoris there is a narrow
> margin between stimulation and irritation. If the un-
> suspecting male partner adheres strictly to marriage
> manual dictum, he is placed in a most disadvantageous
> position. He is attempting proficiency with a technique
> that most women reject with their own automani-
> pulative experience.

Automanipulation of the clitoris means this dreamboat has been switched over to automatic steering. The ballast of self-masturbation for both males and females has been logged as a swell and a breeze since ancient times. It was considered bright work until the Dark Ages came along and hauled in the light, with claims that masturbation was scraping the bottom. These claims, made originally by as-cetic religious fanatics, were hand-me-downs used later by legislators and medical men to anchor self-masturbators with jail sentences, surgery, mental institutions, torturous restraining devices, over-the-side diets, and poisonous "cures." Still, despite threats of one or all of the above, males and females continued to make a grab for their ditty bags and diddle the time away.

But, when self-masturbators were punished by some medical men, there was a whopping difference between a male and a female. The male never got his pecker hacked away as a surgical cure. Tragic to say, there was a splicing difference when it came to the clitoris. And would you believe medical science tagged the surgical removal of the clitoris *and* the minor labia as circumcision! If such surgery was performed on the male genitals, it would decidedly be labeled castration, or partial castration.

In 1956, *Webster's New International Dictionary* defined circumcision as: "The act of cutting off the prepuce, or foreskin, of males, or the internal labia [which includes the clitoris] of females. The circumcision of males is practiced as a religious rite . . . [and] extensively practiced in modern surgery for sanitary measures." Webster, and others, ignored the benefits *and* the reasons behind female "circumcision." Wisely so, since, other than removal of a disease, there are no health-giving benefits from a surgeon's knife hacking away, permanently, all erotic stimulation from a gal's external genital area.

Only recently have manly tomes started to refer to this form of surgery as a clitoridectomy or excision. Interesting that excision, in ecclesiastic terminology, means "expulsion from the church; excommunication."

Clitoridectomy is still a slice out of life in many areas of the world today—where it is still, naturally, called circumcision—especially in certain areas of the Mid and Near East. Here's a quote "excusing" this snatch blocking from a Sudanese male. It appeared as recently as 1962 in a manly tome called *Love in the East.*

. . .circumcision of women releases them from their bondage to sex, and enables them to fulfill their real destiny, as mothers. The clitoris is the basis for female masturbation; such masturbation is common in a hot climate; the spiritual basis of masturbation is fantasy; in fantasy a woman broods on sexual images; such brooding inevitably leads a woman to spiritual infidelity, since she commits adultery in her heart, and this is the first step to physical infidelity, which is the breaker of homes.

This male makes no mention of males having their peckers hacked off for even *fantasizing* about infidelity. And how could he, for if such were the case, there would be no Sudanese in Sudan.

4

WORKING OUT FOR THE ALL-AROUND TOP PRO

For the vagina prostitution is usually a grind. It's a pro-am event where an amateur pays to test his hard muscle against the muscular coordination of a professional who works out by the hour—if not minutes—to keep the vagina in shape. Some cranks claim a pro is in the game just for the dough. Others, probably misfits, say it's a power play all the way. Neither of these theorists realize most pros are in the game for both the power and the dough. And when it comes to top-notch pros, this game is considered a skilled sport. One for which they are willing to put out 110 percent. These top pros have trained their vaginas to shape up and sweat it out, until an amateur feels he has been truly taken. It's a screwy sport and very popular since recorded time began.

And it is because this sport has a long history of skilled, highly trained professionals that we are taking nominations for The Hustler's Hall of Fame.

The professional status of the vagina was recorded as far back as 450 B.C. when the Greek historian Herodotus reported on the pro-am events that took place in the attic of the Tower of Babel. This was not the Tower filled with babbling, presumptuous construction workers but a later model built in 600 B.C. by Nebuchadnezzar. The pros working out in this Tower get the first nomination to the Hall of Fame since Herodotus reports that these skilled pros, who sported on a team called the High Priestesses, turned over all their gate receipts to the Tower's priests as an affirmation of a noble act performed in the honor of their gods.

The bottom line: These were skilled wide receivers who were playing charity events on the up, and up, and up.

Centuries later, amateurs from ancient Egypt are suspected of having sported in Babel with the High Priestesses team. If so, they indeed found It worthy sport since they sponsored similar events in their temples to honor their gods Isis and Osiris. In the next few centuries High Priestesses were sporting in many of the temples in the Middle East. So many, their status changed from isolated teams to a respected league.

The first bad rap the High Priestesses League got was in 13 B.C. when Moses staggered down from the Mount the second time and came up with 603 statutes for all Israelis to abide by. These 603 were in addition to the Big Ten he pulled from a bush on his first ascent. One of the 600 laid down the law banning pro-am events by proclaiming: "There shall be no whore of the daughters of Israel. . . . Thou shall not bring the hire of a whore, or the price of a dog, into the house of the Lord thy God for any vow: for even both of these are abominations unto the Lord thy God."

40

Later, when Moses wanted to prove he still could get in there and pitch, he took unto himself a minor league pro who was tagged a concubine. Mind you though, Moses abided by his ruling because the concubine was an Ethiopian not an Israeli.

Naturally, outside of Israel, Moses bombed. Proof lies in the fact that the High Priestesses League continued to play their pro-am events in temples throughout most of the Middle East, and ancient Greece and Rome for centuries. And why not? These pros were BOX Office.

The first real competition the High Priestesses League came up against was a classy league called the Hetairai, who played out of ancient Greece, the second to be nominated to the Hustler's Hall of Fame.

The key difference between these two leagues was who got the gold—the gate receipts. Whereas, the High Priestesses League turned over their gate receipts to management—the priests who maintained control of the playing field—the Hetairai League refused to play and pay for getting control over the ball. All charity events were kaput. The playing field was now their own individual turf. And this classy league went even further, for not only did the amateur now have to pay top dollar for the privilege of entering an event, he now had to meet the stiff standards required by the Hetairai when they took on a one-to-one sport.

But what made this league such high-class champs was their insistence on a new ruling; they banned the fast ball. And fast play across the board. They cut the pace of the sport to slow—but *very* pleasurable—motion.

And the Hetairai League added another major ruling. All pros who wanted to play in this classy league were not only required to hold their ends up while playing an event, they also were required to make it with their own noodle. No gal could make it in this league if she wasn't well versed in art, politics, philosophy, fashion, music, *and* raking in—on the barrelhead—top bucks for an entry fee. Eventually, this tony league got so liquid that even the government took a slice of their action by levying a whopping tax.

But not to worry, this totally "in" league had It made financially. To check that out, let's audit the till on some of their gate receipts. Were freebies ever handed out? Not even under the table. Hetairai did not believe in freebies. To prove it, Aristaenetus, in his book *Love Letters*, tells us of this response made by a Hetaira when a suitor attempted to woo her with a serenade: "No Hetaira is ever excited by an oboe or captivated by a lyre unless hard cash is brought into the picture. Our only idol [as opposed to the High Priestesses League] is money. We can't be bought with melodies . . ." Ah, but how much hard cash; that's, indeed, the bottom line. Enough for a Brink's haul—500 gold pieces. And when computing the exchange, remember, that's when a gold piece was a PIECE.

As for the long pull, time wise how much time did an amateur get to play? All night, with breakfast thrown in? Don't get too cocky. Clepsydra, a champ Hetaira, kept an hourglass—and one eye peeled counting sand—beside her divan. *And* this clock-watching champ had them standing in line to play by the hour on her up-to-the-minute smoking divan.

Of course the divan was not the only ball field on which these top crotch pros would play. Hetairai liked to prove they were also outdoor sports. Take this quote from another writer, Athenaeus, where he describes one ball park a champ Hetarai enjoyed playing:

> Was not Leontion, that most notorious courtesan, the mistress of Epicurus? Nor did her character change after she began to study philosophy. For in the shady nooks of the Garden [where Epicurus gave his lectures] she submitted [for a price] to the embraces of all his disciples and made no secret of her affair with the Master himself.

Epicurus would know a star pro if anyone did, since it was this philosopher who brought the world the Epicurean theory—the bible for all connoisseurs.

What did the Hetairai look like? Amazons? On the contrary. Most Hetairai were boy slender—like no hips and small breasts (a popular look in ancient Greece where many bisexual males had some queer ideas about big tits and broadlike hips).

Naturally, there is always an exception and this one's exceptional. One of the most beautiful Hetairai, indeed, of all women in ancient Greece, was the pro of pros, Phryne. Her skill for working out with maximum effort for muscling it was so proficient 'twas said no man in Greece could resist taking her on. Add to this, a body so divine that this pro preferred Doing It in the dark because the very sight of her classic form would psyche out any amateur. Her divine bod also saved her neck.

Phryne had toughed it out with so many of the influential men in Athens that she was put on trial for her life as being a menace to the republic. Proud Phryne faced the court as her prosecutor charged her "of being constantly occupied with corrupting the most illustrious citizens of the republic by seducing them from the service of the fatherland." Phryne's defense was a display of her perfect pecs. So psyched out were the judges at this sight that they declared Phryne a divinity and threw her case out of court.

The money for pro-am events rolled in for years for this champ. Gate receipts had reached such a heap, our pro offered to rebuild the walls surrounding Thebes after Alex the Great tumbled them in a siege. With one provision: A plaque on the wall had to read, "Thebes was overthrown by Alexander and rebuilt by Phryne." Her trophy—the symbol of embracing an entire city—was voted down. Could it be because this pro of pros lived—and worked out—in Athens, not in Thebes?

No one, so far, has come up with an audit of Phryne's books, but one Hetaira, Lamina, gives us a clue what a top entry fee could be for an amateur who wanted to take on a champion. Lamina demanded from the King of Macedon 250 talents for a single event—in the balls park of 30,000 smackers. The king, a foul amateur, came up with this humongous amount for an entry fee by levying a soap tax on his citizens. Enraged, his citizens scoured, wondering why their king would even think of sporting with such a filthy pro.

Like any champion league, the Hetairai were competitive pros when it came to hustling for an event. Yet, for those less skilled and down on their luck, most Hetairai were suckers when it came to giving a hand to those pros who failed to tough it out. Take Aspasia, who before she gained top pro status, ran a brothel in Megara. After moving to Athens and taking on Socrates, Alcibiades, and Pericles in pro-am events, this champ opened a training brothel for pros from the minor leagues who had been reduced to street hustling. As part of their training, Aspasia, a skilled orator besides being a champion pro, gave lectures on philosophy and rhetoric. Even the amateurs, many of whom were considered the great thinkers of their time, sat in on these lectures.

Aspasia was so talented and persuasive—in and out of an event—that it is rumored she talked her lover Pericles into allowing her to write the funeral address he made at the outset of the Great Peloponnesian War. In the long range, this funeral address was more apropos for the Athenians, since they lost, eventually, to the Spartans. Historical gossips claim that the eloquence of Aspasia's war cry for Pericles was inspired by her fury after two officers from Megara kidnapped and raped two of the pros working in her brothel. If so, Aspasia was a major contributor to the downfall of Greek civilization, since the fall of the Athenian empire marks the inception of that decline.

The Hustler's Hall of Fame, regretfully, has to refuse the nomination of the world's most famous pro of all—Mary Magdalene. Regretfully because this superstar probably never was a pro, and to top it, she was more than probably a cuckoo. Historians are still arguing about Mary Magdalene's professionalism. This split decision is legit because even the Bible refused to nail Mary as a true pro. The Bible only informs us she was decided favorite of Jesus Christ. Some historians even claim Mary Magdalene was Jesus' secret wife. Other historians go even further and claim that Mary bore Jesus a son and that his lineage has been protected for centuries by secret societies (i.e., Templars and Masons) till the present day. The only certainty about Mary is she's a mystery.

Before the Crucifixion, the only biblical reference to Mary Magdalene is in the Gospel of Luke (8:1–2). But, in a previous verse *and* a chapter before this, reference is made to a "shady lady" who approaches Jesus as he dines with a Pharisee (Luke: 7:37–50, The Authorized King James Version):

> And, behold, a woman in the city, which was a sinner, when she knew that Jesus sat at meat . . . stood at his feet behind him weeping, and began to wash his feet with tears, and did wipe them with the hairs of her head, and kissed his feet and anointed them with the ointment . . . the Pharisee . . . spake within himself, saying, This man, if he were a prophet, would have known who and what manner of woman this is and that toucheth him: for she is a sinner . . . [Jesus] Wherefore I say unto thee, Her sins, which are many, are forgiven; for she loved much: but to whom little is forgiven, the same loveth little . . . And he said to the woman, Thy faith hath saved thee; go in peace.

In the next verse *but* a chapter later, Luke goes on to report:

> And it came to pass afterward, that he went throughout every city and village, preaching and shewing the glad

tidings of the kingdom of God: [a P.R. trip that must have taken at *least* a month or three] and the twelve were with him. And certain women, which had been healed of evil spirits and infirmities, Mary called Magdalene, out of whom went seven devils.

Now, how in sin does this latter reference relate to the nameless foot doctor who went in peace a chapter previous? From the Gospel all we're told about Mary Magdalene's background is that she was healed of evil spirits, infirmities, and seven devils. If a pro, working out, had half those problems, she wouldn't know which end was up.

Asimov's Guide to the Bible says: "To be possessed of the devils, as Mary Magdalene was, would be the sign of what we would today call mental illness. . . . We might much more reasonably consider Mary Magdalene a cured madwoman rather than a reformed prostitute." Well Mary— whatever you were—you just didn't have that pull to make it into the Hustler's Hall of Fame.

And, there was another superstar who also will never get nominated, despite the fact she was, indeed, a true pro. Here's a replay of the foul ball this one-time pro, and a real spoilsport, tried to pull on her fellow teammates. The foul was called in the first quarter of the Middle Ages, historians would say in the late sixth century, when Emperor Justinian I of Byzantium married Theodora, a prostitute. After retiring her professional status, the new empress decided it was time to assist those prostitutes who were reduced to catching balls on the fly. Theodora, impressed with *her* plan for early retirement, commissioned a palatial house for whores. This, unfortunately, was no ordinary whorehouse. The palace was erected on the shores of the Bosphorus, and furnished with the best money could buy. A late-nineteenth-century tome, the *History of Prostitution*, describes the result of Theodora's screw lost idea: ". . . in one night [Theodora] caused five hundred prostitutes in Constantinople to be seized and carried thither. They were kindly treated; their every wish was gratified; but no man entered their asylum. The experiment was a complete failure. Most of the girls committed suicide in their despair, and the remainder soon died of *ennui* and vexation."

When Theodora realized most pros are out for the sport, or at least enjoy bodily contact, she persuaded Justinian to make a severe attempt to protect the plate by tossing everyone out of the game. He decreed that all amateurs caught sporting with a prostitute would be punished by death. All brothel keepers were driven out of town and the pros were assigned either to Theodora's deadly palace or banishment.

The Encyclopaedia Britannica gives only a faint flicker on their scoreboard when it totals up Theodora's previous professional status. It's archaic wording for a 1974 edition— "She [Theodora] became an actress while still young, leading a tainted life that included giving birth to at least one child out of wedlock."

Down the road a few centuries, in the Middle Ages, sports playing in the Western Division, based in the Holy Roman Empire, was up against others out to use their imperial clout to disqualify top-paid playing pros. First up to bat them out of their ball park was Charlemagne, founder of the Holy Roman Empire. He eventually struck out, but the pros hung in there like true champs sweating every pitch. In the twelfth century, second up to bat against the pros was the ground baller Frederick Barbarossa, another Holy Roman Emperor who struck out batting pitches from champions. Both of these holier-than-thou emperors came up with lousy batting averages when it came to getting the pros out of the game.

And small wonder, when the infallible popes, for centuries, had personally sponsored playing hard events with many of the top pros. This brings us to the next top professional league that got nominated to the Hustler's Hall of

Fame—the Courtesan League playing out of Italy. These pros were so classy one unerring pope called one of the league's stars, Imperia, "nobilissium Romae scortum [harlot]."

In addition to class, these pros were skilled at playing politics, for they rarely lost a split decision. And every one of them went all out to win the gold. Indeed, they better have had, because historian Will Durant came up with this account:

> While the simpler prostitutes . . . practiced in brothels, these Roman hetaerae lived in their own homes, entertained lavishly, read and wrote poetry, sang and played music, and joined in educated conversation; some collected pictures and statuary, rare editions and the latest books; some maintained literary salons [a new fad since Gutenberg had just a few decades back invented the printing press] . . . and took classical names . . . Camilla, Polyxena, Penthesilea, Faustina, Imperia, Tuilla.

All of the above have entered the Hustler's Hall of Fame. In fact, most of the Courtesans are perched there. The only ones who don't qualify are those who turned semi-pro; that is, mistresses of popes, cardinals, and other holier-than-thou Romans who restricted a pro's events to playing with a single amateur.

The top hustler among the Courtesans who played during the Renaissance was the champ Tuilla, the daughter of a cardinal and a blond Italian beauty who was skilled in all the arts, especially the art of getting top lira for her skill in the art of making love. Tuilla, along with the other Italian Courtesans, amassed a fortune by restricting her play to seven loaded—with lira—amateurs. One for every night of the week. Events were usually night games since the Courtesan League reserved their days for brain, not bottom, exercises. These seven amateurs were billed for their entry fees once a month and a rain check was never issued if a Courtesan decided to call an event. When an event was called, it usually meant a Courtesan had decided to take on an out of town player—like Henry III, king of France.

Tuilla, for example, so impressed Henry with her match play he took her portrait back with him to France. The French king also must have thought an amateur should reserve his play for only top pros, since Henry ordered, in 1588, all harlots out of Paris in twenty-four hours or face a public whipping and have their heads shaven as a symbol of foul and dirty play.

Minor league players, such as harlots, were getting a lot of catcalls during the fifteenth and sixteenth centuries throughout most of Europe. The word was out that harlots were the cause of an epidemic of syphilis that was devastating pro-am events. Sad to report, many of these catcalls came from amateurs who, after getting or giving a dose, screamed *foul*, as if they were the only ones who were being penalized in the end zone.

Foul play was rarely called on a Courtesan. Usually because she had a king—or three—by his royal balls.

And now we come to the champion hustler of them all and how she bounced her way into the Hall of Fame as a senior citizen. Ninon de Lenclos was a French pro who hustled during three quarters (well, *almost*) of the seventeenth century. She is reputed as "the last of the great courtesans," a title this pro certainly worked out for, since her scorecard lists a total of 4,959 amateurs. (Note: This is not the total of her playing events.)

From an early age Ninon had been in training to measure up for the World Cup award. It helped that she had an "in." Her father was a booking agent—in the trade he was known as a pimp. He was also a talented musician and a big fan of the Epicurean (the best is for the best who are better) philosophy. Before his death, Ninon's father passed on to his beautiful, talented teenaged daughter his idealistic motto for living, his know-how in music, and, best of all, how to hustle for sex.

Ninon, like any future champ, was determined to out-distance all the other pros. From the start of her professional career, Ninon concentrated on erotic arousal in a clutch situation. This won her a ton of future hard-core fans. Ninon, out for the big time, needed a big advance to make her move in Paris. She worked out daily and hourly. By her early twenties, she had enough admirers to finance her as a wide receiver in gay Paree. Once there, for a preliminary heat, she opened her own "salon" and invited the most influential men in France for an evening mixture of mind games and erotic gamboling.

Ninon became a smashing champ. She was a natural crowd pleaser. Also she was tops at hustling, because from opening day on, she never played favorites. Rarely would this champ play the same amateur after a few weeks of events. Ninon was a born switch-hitter. Here's what she had to say about defending her title as a true hustler: "I soon saw that women were put off with the most frivolous and unreal privileges, while every solid advantage was retained by the stronger sex. From that moment on I determined on abandoning my sex and assumed that of men."

So, like any male who hustles in a marketplace for a buck, Ninon went for the top dollar—especially when it came to collecting entry fees from the clergy, who, since early medieval times, had control over most of Europe's cash flow. One priceless example of Ninon's ability to hustle with the best came when the top statesman for all of France—and a cardinal—requested the privilege of playing a single event with her. Like a champion of champions, Ninon upped her entry fee to 50,000 crowns. Ninon shrewdly figured that anyone with the title of cardinal *and* the moniker of Richelieu should be capable of paying top dollar to play with a champ. And then, like a star hustler, Ninon ruthlessly kept the dough and sent in a second-stringer.

Yet this tough pro was known to play an event for the love of it, period. Also, unlike many a pro, she was willing to take on an amateur in a charity event. In those events, she was inclined again to favor the clergy—usually an impoverished monk. To be precise, one scorekeeper came up with a total of 439 stir-crazy monks.

Yet, in the long snap, after forty years of playing events, the champ discovered what she enjoyed most was giving good theater. So, at the age of sixty, this skilled pro decided to open her own private training camp. But this time, the training program wasn't for the education of other pros. Instead, Ninon decided it was high time the amateurs learned that gouging was not permitted.

For the next five years, pro Ninon, in an all-out effort, trained rookies how to "go for it." She probably would have continued till the day she died if fate hadn't one day decided to turn thumbs down on this champion's play. It's a tragic story. So tragic, some claim it has to be unreal. True or not, Ninon did close up her training camp without giving notice.

The story goes: One day a friend asked Ninon to take on a young amateur, a soldier, who had fallen passionately in love with her. After a brief meeting with the soldier, Ninon, without giving him a reason, refused the rookie entry. Repeated pleas to prove his love were rebuffed by this usually openhearted champ. Driven mad with his frustrated passion, the rookie implored Ninon to return his ardor. The old pro then, uncharacteristically, replied: "Look at me. It is sixty-five years since I came into this world. So you think at this age I can listen to declarations of love? Can you not see your passion is ridiculous?"

Tragically, the rookie could not see Ninon in any other light than the flame of his own passion. He called once more.

And, finally, Ninon was forced to reveal why she had refused him entry—he was her own natural son by a former amateur, after playing a pro-am event.

The rookie, stunned, whispered, twice, "Mother," and fled into her garden. There the young soldier braced his sword and flung his body on it.

After his death, Ninon refused to train. But like a born pro, she did play private events until the day she died. She was a worn-to-a-nub, blissful eighty-five—and one dynamite champ.

There are those who might well protest the decision to close the nominations for the Hustler's Hall of Fame after Ninon was certified as the champ of all the pros, since after an audit there were other pros who hustled hard and brought in more bucks than this champ. The Italian countess Nicchia de Castiglione charged a million francs for an entry fee; Kitty Fisher, a London pro, charged 100 guineas; another London pro, Laura Bell, hustled a maharaja for 250,000 pounds; in Paris a British pro, Cora Bell, got 10,000 francs for an entry; and in Spain a pro called La Belle Otero is said to have made $25 million during her lifetime—but then she lived to the age of 97.

A quote from Otero explains the difference between an ordinary hustler, no matter how much she gained from hustling, and the champs who made it into the Hall of Fame. Otero was asked before she died what she would have done with the $20 million she threw away as a compulsive gambler during her lifetime. The Spanish pro replied, "I might have endowed a university for prostitutes. Think of the variety of classes we might have had."

The champs in the Hall of Fame were more considerate of their sport. They believed in helping other pros get ahead and were concerned about all forms of education to improve the game, and those same rules were applied to the amateurs. That's what makes them *the* champs.

Difficult to predict whether in the future the Hall of Fame will reopen nominations. Its been close to three centuries since a champ of such caliber has come along. As far back as 1853—150 years after Ninon's death—Gustave Flaubert predicted we had seen the last of these champs when he wrote, "My only complaint about prostitution is that it is a myth. The kept woman has invaded the field of debauchery, just as the journalist has invaded poetry; everything is becoming mongrelized. There are no more courtesans, just as there are no more saints . . ."

Of course not everyone can be a champion pro—or a saint. The sport goes on and the pros continue to carry the ball. Over the centuries, thousands of nicknames have cropped up in nations all over the world to glorify—and slam—these dedicated pros.

For those who like to poke around, here's a list of some several hundred names given to pros—and mind you, it's just the opening half.

EUPHEMISMS AND SYNONYMS FOR PROSTITUTES AND THE FEMALE GENITAL AREA

It's a Concession	*It's a Concession (cont.)*
Raspberry tart	Black meat
Beef steak	Tenderloin madam
Hot mutton	Coffee grinder
Artichoke	Bun
Sardine	Stew
Rabbit pie	Shank
Tomato	Bit of mutton
Laced mutton	Shad
Biscuit	Cocktail
Shrimp	Tart
Hot beef	Pastry

It's a Concession (cont.)
Gin
Sweetmeat
Cake
Fork
Swallow-cock

Foul Line
Barrack hack
Guttersnipe
Fallen woman
Bed-faggot
Freak trick
Gutter slut
Lewd woman
No better than she should be
Tricking broad

Most-Valuable Player
Thoroughbred
Pro
Sportswoman
Thrill dame
Battler
Sister of mercy
Weekend warrior
Receiver general
Knock-em-down
Princess of the pavement
Trooper
Prostitute
Bunter

Stop Watching
Fast fanny
Speedy sister

Stop Watching (cont.)
Half by halfer
Early door
Six to four
Two to four
Hurry whore
Mistress quickly
Quickie
Fling dust
Vent renter
Toll hole
Notch broad
Nigh enough

Second-String
Roger's wife
Covent Garden nun
Hobby-horse
Lost lady
Sporting-girl
Lift-skirts
Nymph of the pavement
B-girl
Mixer
Sitter
C-girl
Bit of stuff
Working girl
Demirep
Go-between
Convenient
Housekeeper

Heave To
Loose fish

Heave To (cont.)

Mermaid
Ferry
Flash-tail
Flipper
Harpie
Ho
Fish

Goalie

Bachelor's wife
Spinster
Housekeeper
Dutch widow
Scarlet sister
Suburban
Tail
Red-light sister
Piper's wife
Puritan
Nun
Occupant
Bawdy basket

On the Road

Fly by night
Baggage
Overnight bag
Hunt about
Bicycle
Trip
Woman about town
Foreskin hunter
Omnibus
Road

On the Road (cont.)

Picker-up
Cab moll
Cannon woman
Hotel hotsy

Losing Streak

Stale
Brush-scrubber
Window tapper
Twidget
Jaded Jenny
Hide
Academician
Sit at show window

Catcalls

Animal
Harlot
Ass peddler
Alley cat
Dead meat
Cow
Garbage can
Dog
Pig
Rattlesnake
Bat
Fuck freak
Floozie
Garbage lady
Gook
Roach
Mort wop-apace
Needle woman

Catcalls (cont.)

Carrion
Whore
Bitch
Wasp
Blimp
Cock-eyed Jenny
Blow
Nit

Fit to Play

Scrub
White apron
On the game
Fresh and sweet
Choose
Saturday to Monday
Perfect lady
Warm member
Dasher
Pure
Fit for company

Mascot

Bear
Lioness
Tiger
Moose
Dragon
Toby

Promoter

Twofer
Hustler
Dress for Sal

Promoter (cont.)

Entertainer
Crack salesman
Belter
Hype
Piece of trade
Pavement pounder
Pintle merchant
Hooker
Privateer
Saleslady
Trader
Cruiser
Hello dearie
Mrs. Warren's Profession
Get the rent
Apartment to let
Company girl

Foul Call

Woman of loose morals
Sinner
Punchable nun
Common sewer
Forgotten woman
Whore-bitch
Sin sister
Poker breaker
Sample of sin
Outlaw
Bludger
Bad girl
Pagan
Weed monkey
Vice-sister

Painted cat
Low heel
Fleabag
Glueneck

Equipped
Kid-leather
Jack whore
Carry-knave
Tarry rope
Mattress
Trull
Flax-wench
Treddle
Poker climber
Twigger
Brimstone
Article
Bint
Mat
Nest-cock
Brass nail
Wapping-dell
Scuffer
Kittock
Holer
Bulker
Skrunt

Benched
Split-arse mechanic
Blister
Lusher

Beat moll
Unfortunate
Blue foot
Hot rocks
Doorkeeper
Stiff-quean
Thrugmoldy
Spoff-skins
Shongler
Frail sister
Bug
Flapper
Deadly nightshade
Cracked pitcher
Claptrap
Dusty butt
Hip flipper
Impure
A mystery
Rag
Treble cleft
Loose-bodied Gown
Old Rip

Night Game
Nymph of darkness
Night piece
Nocturnal
Night walker
Night shade
Nightbird
Night Hunter
Night jobber
Lady of the evening

Lineup

Juanita
Madame Vans
Jane
Delilah
Athanasian wench
Bimmy
Jezebel
Dulcinea
Magdalene
Sadie Thompson
Madam Ran
Maude
Daughter of Eve
Maggie
Maid Marian
Rory O'More
Lady
Call girl
Blouza-Linda
Columbine
Judy
Incognita
Kate

Cup Race

Barnacle
Sloop of war
Broken oar
Sailor's delight
Fore and Aft
Sailor bait
She sails
Boat and oar
Fireship

Cup Race (cont.)

Bit of muslin
Bucket broad
Shoreditch fury
Scupper
Flag aboard

Unaffiliated

Freelancers
Sidewalk Suzie
Give-and-take girl
Lift-skirt
Hip peddler
Courtesan
Working for herself
Liberated
Street sister
Blower
Gamester
Suburb-sister
Tail peddler
Single woman
Lease piece
Sunday girl
Flesh peddler
Free ride
Green goods
Two-bit hustler
Moonlighter
Lay
Skirt
Street walker

Off-Line

Pug-nasty

Off-Line (cont.)

Hump
Erring sister
Bangster
Screw
Filth
Dead picker
Trick babe
Daughter
Mother
Dirty puzzle
Mob
Jilt
Stem siren
Jaga-bat
Stram
Vice-sale
Trickster
Virtue after
Public ledger
Nag
Shake
Tumble
Wapping-dell
Scrousher
Barber's chair

Regional Title

Sisters of the bank
Model
Nestle cock
A sport
Whoopie wenches
Painted woman
Girls at ease

Regional Title (cont.)

Loose Love ladies
Fancy woman
Charity
Broadway broad
Purse finder
Pleasure lady
Woman of accommodating
  morals
Lady of leisure
Joy girl
Lady of expansive sensibility
Woman of pleasure
Gay piece
Give-and-take girl
Tweat
Masseuse
Gay woman
Mixer
Love lady
Perfect lady
Hot picker
Merry legs

Farm Team

Goose
Livestock
Pheasant
Soiled dove
Bunny
Cat
Crow
Owl
Moth
Badger

Farm Team (cont.)	Sports Abroad (cont.)
Wheat belt	Puta
Rustle	Anonyma
Nightingale	Bona roba
Night hawk	Scolopendria
Minx	Poncess
Partridge	Nafkeh
Brown Bess	Mauks
Malee root	Noffugur
Bird	Chromo
Quail	Puttock
Chick	Kife
Fly	Pynnage
Cattle	Grisette
Hay bag	Quaedam
Burlap sister	Soss-brangle
Goat-milker	Case vrow
Stallion	Paphian
	Quandong
Sports Abroad	Cro
Fille de joie	Nymphe du pave
Meretix	Quiff
Palliasse	Croshabelle
Dant	Concilatrix

Nicknames, though, do little to describe what the sport is all about—that would take another book. But some quotes that have come down through time give us a snapshot of what it is like playing for and in the world's favorite ball park. The perspective for the following quotes comes from many areas: the players—pro and amateur, the reporters, the critics, and the booster club.

It's a business to do pleasure with you. (Anonymous pro)

No woman is born a whore and any woman can become one. (Polly Adler)

I'm hungry. Let's go to a brothel and get some broth. (Mark Twain)

He: "How did a smart girl like you wind up in this business?" (99 percent of the amateurs)

She: "Just lucky I guess." (The majority of pros)

I may say I have never had a preferred lover . . . an amiable man who has loyally offered me his arms, his love, and his money has every right to think and call himself my favorite lover, my lover for an hour . . . That is how I understand the business. (Pro, Cora Pearl)

. . . but he that keepeth company with harlots spendeth his substance. (Proverbs 29:3)

Prostitutes provide something special: a complete illusion for the male. (Jennifer James)

. . . at bottom a mad and irresistible craving for excitement, a serious and wilful revolt against the monotony of commonplace ideals, and the uninspired drudgery of daily life. (A. Sherwell, 1897)

. . . for between those who sell themselves to prostitution and those who sell themselves to marriage, the only difference is in price and duration of the contract. (Maro)

To all the girls who took my money and took me into their lives for an hour or a day, good, bad, young and old, plain and pretty alike. (Martin O'Brien)

I am not a psychiatrist, but I am convinced that sex is not as important as we tend to make it. (The Happy Hooker, Xaviera Hollander)

. . . prostitutes must be put on the same level as artists. Both use their gifts and talents for the joy and the pleasure of others, and, as a rule, for payment. (Anonymous)

A woman's body is without price, is an axiom of prostitution. The money placed in the hands of her who procures the satisfaction of sexual desire is not the price of the act, but an offering which the priestess of Venus applies to her maintenance. (Bernaldo de Quiros and Llanas Aquilaniedo)

The cheerful, skillful and artistically accomplished *hetaira* frequently stands as an ideal figure in opposition to the intellectually uncultivated wife banished to the interior of the house. (H. Schurtz)

Women have the right to be or not to be prostitutes. (Prostitutes Rights Contingent)

It is perhaps a perverse taste, but I like prostitution— and for its own sake, independently of what lies underneath. My heart has never failed to pound at the sight of one of those provocatively dressed women walking in the rain under the gas lamps, just as the sight of monks in their robes and knotted girdles touches some ascetic, hidden corner of my soul. Prostitution is a meeting point of so many elements—lechery, frustration, total lack of human relation, physical frenzy, the clink of gold—that a glance into its depths makes one giddy and teaches one all manner of things. It fills you with such sadness! And makes you dream so of love! Ah, elegy-makers, it is not on ruins that you should lean, but on the breasts of these light women. (Who else but Flaubert)

All cats look the same in the dark. (A slob)

My body is my own and what I do with it is nobody else's concern. (Anonymous pro)

Despite certain old wives tales, a prostitute's vagina isn't made any differently—and *might* not work any differently—than the vagina of any other nonprofessional female. Nor, according to another tale, does the vagina wear out—or down—from daily, even hourly, use. But it does, according to some hot-air balloonists, get frozen—to the degree of frigid—or overheated—to the point of, grab this one, repetitive volcanic eruptions—which, in the fiction of science, has been tagged as nymphomania.

5

TEMPERATURE FORECAST FOR VAGINAL ZONES

What's the climate like down there? For most, past and present, the answer pops up, "A first class trip to Paradise!" Still, in the past century or more, reports have polarized the *healthy* vagina, a volcano in the heave of persistent eruptions, from a submerged, impenetrable iceberg.

Let's take a shovel to ice and ashes, to dig our way back to Paradise. It's a long haul. We start chipping ice in the sexual repression of the Victorian Age, then sweat in out in the hot beds of the twentieth-century sexual revolution.

In the mid-sixteenth century, *frigid* was a unisex English term for those sexually disabled. Three centuries down, frigidity became a medical, soon layman's (yes, pun intended), catchall term for the inorgasmic, the sterile, or the sexually unresponsive vagina. With this frigid sexist nineteenth-century definition came an avalanche of snow that eventually buried untold thousands of vaginas. Still, only fair to add, all received a "healthy" signal from those medicine men who dedicated themselves to the science of weather forecasting in vaginal zones.

Dare we ask how these scientists discovered, after thousands of centuries of tropical hype, that the normal, healthy vagina was frigid? No, because it remains their secret to this day. For an answer, all we can do is reexamine their vaginal reports, sightings, findings, and forecasts.

In the animal world, it has been known since the time of primitive shepherds that the vagina has its torpid/torrid seasons. That the "heat" season varied from one animal species to the next has been recorded down through the ages in weighty tomes and scatological verse.

From *The Slang of Venery*, here is a seventeenth-century English calendar dating—for a beastly few—the blessing of a heat season:

> Season of Beasts, a Heart or Buck begins at the end of Fencer-Month, 15 days after Midsummer-day, and lasteth till Holyrood-day, The Fox till Christmas, and lasteth till the Annunciation of the blessed Virgin, The Hinde or Doe at Hollyrood-day, till Candlemass, The Roe-buck at Easter, till Michaelmass, The Roe at Michaelmass till Candlemass, The Hare at Michaelmass, till the end of February, The Wolf from Christmas, till the Annunciation of the blessed Virgin, The Boar at Christmas, and continues to the Purification of our Lady.

That humans were not restricted to a sexual season has to have been computed by man, common sense tells us, no later than year two on his/her primitive calendar. Heat, no heat, no one had to give a fig. Then came Victorian England and with it, science's climatic control of vaginal zones. Suddenly, there appeared on the medical horizon, which was illogically deep, broad areas of glacial submerged masses; that is, vaginal icebergs.

It should come as no surprise that Victorian males did not cheer at medical sightings of healthy frigid vaginas. They suspected, with good cause, that what the medicine men were scanning was an icebound cure for the plague of the pox—now recognized by science as the third, often fatal, stage of syphilis. For, despite the scars from a plague of pox, sex was *in,* after centuries of religious sexual put-downs. In England it was ball time.

Take this analysis from a continental visitor to England in 1700: "the women of this country are much given to sensuality, to carnal inclinations, . . . [and other loose et ceteras]."

But, as a marketing device, you can't beat fear. And the Victorian lady was soon blanketed with the snow job that the frigid vagina was the proper, and the healthy vagina. For the sexually insecure (a statistic that magically, and tragically, escalated during the sexual repression of the Victorian Age), frigid sightings in vaginal zones brought a welcome frost-freeing relief. Here, finally, was medical proof it was both healthy and wise to pull your flap at the mere thought of entry into the depth of this frigid terrain.

Was the world facing a sexual Ice Age? Surely not.

English physicians sighted healthy icebergs only in Anglo vaginas, and those were usually in ladies of the upper class. But icebergs do float. Soon physicians in Italy, Germany, and the United States lowered themselves to discover their own sightings. The *healthy* news here was: Not only was vaginal frigidity spreading, it was no longer class-conscious—well almost not; that is, peasants and their ilk were cursed with the unhealthy immunity of illiteracy and an expanding Industrial Age with voracious need for a limitless working class.

As for the rest of the world: Alien reports and forecasts of frigidity in vaginal zones were considered fucking unreal. Here, males looked down with pride, then wondered piteously, what sort of foreign tool could possibly turn a vaginal area into an iceberg. Far worse, their use of scientific statistics to maintain a frigid climate control of vaginas had to be *the* ultimate foreign fucking end.

In their common sensible world, the vaginal area was still tropic, lush, and indeed a paradise. But, in those nations pumping frigid forecasts, males and females soon became brainwashed by the new science: healthful vaginal frozen forecasts with readouts by respected medical scientists.

Ah, do we hear a hiss "What a snow job!" from today's smart asses, the sexually enlightened? Wait. Bank your fire till we get further down and check out contemporary reports on vaginal meltdown!

The first sighting of the avalanche burying untold thousands of vaginas snowballed in England in 1857. It was reported by physician William Acton, who, bless his balls, sighted the healthy Ice Age for vaginal areas with his finding: ". . . that the majority of women (happily for society) are not very much troubled with sexual feelings of any kind." And, his clincher: ". . . those who claimed otherwise, male or female, were casting vile aspersions on these frigid saints."

"Frigid saints" to thousands of women saddled with unskilled lovers *and* Victorian sexual repression *and* syphilis could only ring god bless those automatic ice makers.

Not surprising, it soon became popular to cool it, man; pop a halo; turn your temp down below to minus zero; and lie down, frozen shut, knowing, finally, you would be recognized for what you were: a saint—true, not your martyred one, but what the hell. As for their numb-to-the-bone mates, they were left to pray, in shriveled hope, for the return of springtime and a corking thaw.

Sorry mates, this was only the tip of her monstrous iceberg.

Soon Acton's frigid sighting got backup from a medical encyclopedia, and with it, a subliminal mention for the saintly lady. Read it and weep: ". . . that a mucous fluid is sometimes found in coition from the internal organs and the vagina is undoubted; but this only happens in lascivious women, or such as live luxuriously." With this arid finding, in a prestigious medical text, it figures dew-point averages dried up in vaginal areas faster than you can rip off Frosty the Snowman. For what lady in class-act Victorian England wanted to be labeled a sweating, though well-paid, whore?

To lock it up, anonymous Snowman continued that his research proved 90 percent of all frigid vaginas could be laid to congenital influence. For a clue, what we're looking at is: Frigidity spreads from vagina to vagina—males might not be immune to frost, but they were blooming, safe from sprouting a frigid sex organ. This certainly proves out, since a male has yet to be found who ever looked below to find an iceberg between his thighs.

After these frigid forecasts, the big snow drifted across to the European continent with a forecast for blizzard conditions around the globe. From an Italian medical perspective, tropic vaginas, worldwide, were swept away in one devastating avalanche. Wrap yourself up against this forecast from an Italian physician who found that *all* women are "naturally and organically frigid."

In Germany, an abnormal sighting was reported when a physician recorded: Frigidity is "far more complex. In the normal woman, especially of the higher social classes, the sexual instinct is acquired not inborn; when it is inborn, or awakes by itself there is abnormality. Since women do not know this instinct before marriage, they do not miss it when they have no occasion in life to learn it."

But the screwiest frigid report/forecast came out of the United States. You may well shudder after reading this 1907 statistic from Manhattan: "75% of the married women in New York are afflicted with . . . frigidity, and . . . it is on the increase; it is rare, however . . . among Jewish women." (A *brachah* to be sure.)

Irrespective of race, back in Germany, Sigmund Freud reported a woman frigid, no matter how climactic her performance, if (mind you, big IF) she did not, during *coitus*, achieve full sexual satisfaction *vaginally*. Were we now spying the eye of the frigid storm when we read of Freud's sighting? If nothing else, we are looking at nailing the climactic vagina to the wall as a cure-all for a frozen sex life, but *only* during coitus.

For nonfrigid gals, this was a snow scene beyond belief. And for most frozen ones, Freud's vaginal sighting was classified as a mirage, since it was a rare saint that knew where—other than down there somewhere—her vagina was. But even more disturbing for those saintly frozen women was Freud's blanket report that frigidity was caused by guilt. However, could a gal be frozen with guilt when she was lying, blessed, as a Victorian saintly sexless saint?

Freud was not a popular forecaster. He was considered unscientific, especially on the medical scene, with his hammering away at frigidity as the basic cause for neurosis. For the medicine men, it was neurosis that was a snow job beyond belief.

But the pendulum swings, and frigid medical forecasts were on the wane, partially due to communication's expansion in the early twentieth century and partially due to a decrease in syphilis cases after five centuries. So before we analyze the Freudian avalanche, let's look at early-twentieth-century reports from countries where a vaginal trip was a sure ticket to a tropic thirsty paradise.

In Arabia, where frigidity was nonexistent, a report sighted: "The longing of the woman for the penis is greater than that of a man for the vulva." From Russia, this overall report sighted: "A girl . . . cannot resist the ever stronger impulses of sex beyond the twenty-second year . . . and if she cannot do so in natural ways she adopts artificial ways." In Scandinavia, there was this seductive sighting: "We hardly hear anyone talk of a woman being seduced, simply because the lust is at worst with a woman, who, as a rule, is the seducing party."

With these sightings, we could read a cold front and a warm front were about to clash—the result: clouds over vaginal zones, but the *possibility* of a cleansing, refreshing, warming rain.

Take this observation from a skeptic on local forecasts of vaginal activity. Havelock Ellis, an English sexologist and a noted researcher into global vaginal zones, said:

> We thus find two opinions widely current: one, of world-wide existence and almost universally accepted in those ages and centers in which life is lived almost nakedly, according to which the sexual impulse is stronger in women than in men; another, now widely prevalent in many countries [remember Ellis speaks from an empire where the sun never sets], according to which the sexual instinct is distinctly weaker in women, if indeed, it may not be regarded as normally absent all together. A third view is possible: it may be held that there is no difference at all . . . in that men and women are equal in sexual impulse.

Was the Arctic wind switching? And did windbags flapping over frozen vaginas pick it up? You should remember, the natural state of a windbag is limp. If strategically placed, a windbag sucks air in and flaps away announcing to all the sexual weather conditions, from its mighty peak down to that lowly valley. But the vagina, in this Ice Age, was the lowest valley of all. To get a wind switch down there, you would need more than a windbag; you would need a trusty weathercock.

What to do with thousands upon thousands of frigid vaginas? A cure had to be found and like true-blue medicine men, the search was on for a trusty weathercock. Some leaned toward Havelock Ellis, but for most, Ellis' signals coming from all points of the globe were thought too far out for reliable vaginal forecasting. That was when medicine men refocused on those frigid reports signaled for decades by Sigmund Freud. As a weathercock, wasn't it Freud who signaled that the Arctic storm that blew in saintly vaginas could possibly be a mirage? Mind you, a legit mirage, after all, at the time we were all looking at blizzard conditions.

As a trusty weathercock, Freud was the salvation of medicine men. True his signals were odd, but then, so were their frigid saints.

With Freud you had to focus—in. It wasn't vaginal *zones* that were frigid; it was the vagina, period. And the reason it was frigid was that saint you were kneeling to was actually frozen in an inoperable incestuous fantasy. Fucked saints were subconsciously fucked-up over their papas. How does that grab you for a fantasy snow job?

Hey, mates, you lapped it up. First, it wiped the icy saints—a wasting bore as a challenge down below. Second, you could blame frigidity on your father-in-law. Third, Freud claimed frigidity was curable; with those frozen saints, forget it.

As Freud signaled it, all a frozen gal had to do was talk it out with a medicine man—now tagged Freudian analyst—admit where her fantasy was at, then wait for the temperature in her vagina to heat up and melt the ice blockage. So how come it didn't work?

Freud and Freudian analysts were locked to a scientific theory that frigid patients were individually, and subconsciously, the source for their inorgasmic vaginas. That medical science had brainwashed, subconsciously, a majority of these frigid patients was ignored in Freudsville—a possible answer for why medical science ignored, till recent times, questioning Freud's theory as a cure-all for frigid vaginas.

No more. Today Freudian scholars debate: Why was it Freud ignored—time and again—his frigid patients' "remarkable claims that one parent had attempted or achieved their seduction as children. Freud then made another [now a debated career step] discovery—that these childhood seductions had *in fact* never occurred, but were at first fantasies, and then the reversal of a desired role." (Author's emphasis in quote from the *Encyclopaedia Britannica*, 1974.)

Their worthy debate should also examine: Why did medical science ignore a medical fact, that the Freudian theory on incestuous childhood fantasies did not cure frigidity? (Not to mention that this guru on sexual satisfaction was an acknowledged celibate most of his married life remains a Freudian sweep under the scientific rug to this day.) And why, for several decades, did medicine men, now on a humane search to warm vaginal zones, back up this weathercock's misguided signals of where frigidity was at?

Take a read on these Freudian frigidity signals published in 1951 by Dr. Edmund Bergler, a staunch support for orthodox Freudian forecasts:

> Under frigidity we understand the incapacity of woman to have a vaginal orgasm during intercourse. It is of no matter whether the woman is aroused during coitus or remains cold, whether excitement is weak or strong, whether it breaks off at the beginning or end, slowly or suddenly, whether it is dissipated in preliminary acts, or has been lacking from the beginning. The sole criterion of frigidity is absence of vaginal orgasm.

The vagina had to carry the weight of ice for a shaming amount of time, and—as programmed—do it without cracking.

When did the medicine men indicate a thaw was sighted? A century after Acton's frigid saints were sighted in 1857. Frigidity *slowly* melted down to a new medical term, *sexual anesthesia*, which *slowly* evaporated into sexual inadequacy or incompetency—the cause cited as organic, relationship, or psychological, or a combination of two, or all three. That the latter two were, for a century, in a majority of "frigidity" cases, brought on by medical forecasting is a wipe in most medical histories.

For the next decade reports on healthy vaginal temperatures read in the normal range. But, in the heat of the sexual revolution of the 1970s, hot air began blowing over the vaginal zone. Some of this hot air was blown by a new breed of medical scientists—sex therapists—some by overheated males and females sweating it out, holding up their own organs in the ever-expanding explosion of a sexual revolution. The hotter vaginal reports got, the healthier the forecast for vaginal zones, till sexual meltdown was sighted. And, naturally, the core of this meltdown was, that sucker, the vagina—specifically the multiorgasmic vagina.

This overactive volcano, bubbling away with threats of persistent orgasmic eruptions, was sighted as a menace to the balance of nature—that is, male organs, in the majority, physiologically programmed for *their* single orgasmic eruption. Drained mates reported they couldn't come up with enough stoppers, and that persistent vaginal eruptions were threatening to envelop them. And for those staunch mates that did hang in there, menacing reports soon came. *Meltdown!*

On top of it all, females reported the steam from atmospheric pressure was getting to them. That the healthy vagina should be having orgasmic eruption after eruption, and was capable of a hundred eruptions—all in one sex encounter—became too hot for many a gal to cope with. Some turned frigid at the thought. Others reported laying there lying, mentally/physically exhausting themselves, performing fake eruptions to keep up with "healthy" vaginas. Others complained that to score, one now felt a pressure to keep a score of their eruptions. The countdown alone—from healthy reports of 100—zapped them.

And who were the vaginal forecasters of the 1970s? A few medicine men, but, for the main, media—all forms of media. Vaginal forecasting was especially hot in the television media of the United States. On talk shows, the talk of the town became in-depth reports from owners of volcanic vaginas—bubbling over with their news that the more orgasmic eruptions, the better for them; and not unheard of, piteous recognition of their mate's weakness for meltdown.

But the real media stars were the sex therapists with their mouths full of statistical data on what was normal, healthy, and satisfying for all questioning mates, with most sex therapists zeroing in on the hot, but *never* overheated, vagina.

What does it all boil down to? For the majority, too much heat, as with frigidity, proves oppressive.

Is there a healthy solution on the vaginal horizon? A possible relief from the heat, yes; healthy, no. As of this printing, the plague of fatal AIDS is reported as cooling off the sex scene. The cool was first reported in the gay world after thousands of AIDS deaths were attributed to the practice of anal sex. Now the cool has spread into the heterosexual world with reports that AIDS is also transmitted via vaginal sex (a transfer previously recorded in African nations and Haiti).

By 1991, we are now looking at an ominous forecast: In a speech delivered on January 19, 1987, the Surgeon General of the U.S. Public Health Service predicted that there would be a nine-fold increase in the total number of AIDS victims by the end of 1990 (a total close to 270,000), but the increase in AIDS cases involving heterosexual persons will increase about 20-fold. The statistics at the time of his speech read "30,000 cases, with 4 percent of *all reported* cases between heterosexual men and women who are not I.V. drug abusers." In an August 1987 interview with *Washington Post* reporters, American physician Jonathan Mann, the head of the AIDS program for the World Health Organization in Geneva, is quoted as saying: "In the U.S., estimates suggest that there are between 400,000 and 4 million infected Americans." And with this broad span of estimates it is difficult to get a true picture on infection rates. To the question "Is the AIDS epidemic spreading as fast as early predictions?" Mann responded, ". . . we have not yet developed the tools to answer that question adequately. National estimates of the number of infected persons have been criticized severely . . . on the ground that they have been made on the basis of relatively little information."

Whatever the statistic reads in truth, until a cure for AIDS is found, those who practice unsafe sex are flirting with fatal sex.

Are we looking at possible panic? Could be. For a caution, take a read on an editorial (*The New York Times*) that appeared Nov. 7, 1986, under the headline "DON'T PANIC, YET, OVER AIDS," which, under media forecasting, came up with: "The likelihood of transmission in a single sexual encounter seems small. . . . The smartest thing now is to resist exaggerated fears of heterosexual transmission—and to fund more drug-treatment programs."

For another caution, there is this concluding quote from a letter protesting the *Times* editorial: "We are convinced significant heterosexual spread of AIDS virus is occurring now in the U.S." The letter was signed by Nobel laureate Dr. David Baltimore and Dr. Sheldon Wolff, cochairs of a six-month AIDS study for the National Academy of Sciences.

For a final caution: It is currently estimated that 25 to 75 percent of those infected with the virus will develop AIDS in the next seven years, and these figures have escalated from a previous estimate of 10 percent. In the United States alone, it is currently estimated that from 1.5 to 3 million Americans have already been infected by the virus. Worldwide, U.S. Surgeon General C. Everett Koop predicts that if AIDS goes unchecked by the year 2000, this fatal virus could kill 100 million people, dwarfing all previous world epidemics. When one considers that the Black Death during the Middle Ages killed 25 million, we understand Koop was talking *serious* sex when he dropped this statistic in a speech to college students in January 1987, urging students to use condoms (no guarantee for 100 percent prevention) and practice monogamy (less guarantee for those previously into playing the field, since the incubation period for AIDS could be as long as fourteen years).

But the focus here, though unreal, was the "healthy" vagina as perceived by medicine men or laypersons. Unreal because medical science took a tragic time to come to terms with the vagina. Frigidity today is a medical term out of the past—the inhuman past. As for laymen, unreal fears of meltdown from overheated vaginas are finally melting. For the layperson, the orgasmic countdown now is a healthy "What works for me is what's real."

So, what is the climate like down there after a century of climactic control? For your health and the health of the vagina, stick with Paradise.

You will never be swept away by atmospheric pressure again.

Or will you?

Is there a fiscal "love season" for humans? Apparently so. For a fiscal accounting, balance if you will this quote from the 1974 publication of the *Encylopaedia Britannica* comparing birth peaks for primates in the wild and captivity, and a wrap-up of global birth peaks in humans:

> In the wild, birth seasons are closely correlated with the prevailing climate. . . . In captivity, under both laboratory and zoo conditions, anthropoids breed throughout the year with little evidence of seasonality. Even in man there is evidence of high birth peaks. In Europe, the highest birth rates are reached in the first half of the year, and in countries in the Southern Hemisphere in the second half. This may, however, be a cultural rather than ecological phenomenon, for marriages in certain western countries reach a peak in the closing weeks of the fiscal year. . . .

The fiscal year varies from nation to nation. We invite you to check out yours. Then, do a flowchart of your sexual activity; compare that with your personal fiscal ending; then, compare all with his/her fiscal ending. You will come up with an interface for SOP (Standard Operating Procedure) to resolve all future atmospheric pressure.

And that's the bottom line for low-level management.

6

ONE ORGASM, TWO ORGASMS, THREE ORGASMS—MORE, MORE, MORE!

Delight the orgasmic gourmet in you and savor a variety of recipes that have satiated the vagina, via multiorgasms, for hundreds of centuries on our globe. From ancient times to the present, many gourmets, both female and male, have pitched right in and created surefire recipes that will bring The Vessel to a boiling point, then a simmer, then a boiling point, over and over again—without destroying the delicate flavor of each individual orgasm. Unrest assured, these timeless recipes are the horn of plenty when it comes to numbers, variety, and delirious delicious feasting.

Inclined to pig out on orgasms? Go for it. If you

really love to pack it in, you gain an added plus—actually the beauty of a minus—for while loaded with starch these creamy recipes have zilch calories. Semen combined with vaginal juices is the diet pop for the ages. But remember mates, if there is not enough starch, it's first come, first served.

And, if you're into multiorgasmic feasting, keep in mind this is never a fast-refreshment operation. These feasts require thoughtful preparation, sensitive creativity, time-consuming execution, and a potful of stirring.

Those addicted to a heat-and-get-served process, are fated to get the sticky end of the stick when it comes down to experiencing a vaginal orgasmic feast. Vessels are made to boil, and boil, and boil again, without losing moisture, if proper timing is there.

The novice should take note of these basic guidelines for laying on an orgasmic feast: A vaginal orgasmic gourmet never sinks to the use of an additive. Preservatives, naturally, are questionable. Before putting meat in the pot— oops! vessel—it should be checked to see whether it has been tenderized, and a true gourmet will pull up stakes before putting any *thing* into The Vessel that looks old, wilted, or—that real curdler—moldy. Likewise, if any *thing* looks blue around the gills, a gal should remember she has other fish to fry.

Finally, the no-no of all no-no's: Don't even *think* of stuffing the meat in and turning your timer on.

Now, some pointers on that pot of pots, *The* Vessel. Vessels come in a variety of sizes—difficult for some to fathom. Regardless of its size, The Vessel is fully capable of accommodating any size tool that proves useful for a complete stirring.

It would profit the budding gourmet to examine a Vessel close up; after you blow the hair out of your eyes, you will note it has a ticklish knob. This knob should *never* be ignored (some dry engineer tagged it the clitoris). It is documented that no amount of delicate, mind now *delicate*, tinkering with this knob has ever spoiled an orgasmic feast. For most orgasmic recipes, tinkering with the knob is done during the preheating stage, which can vary anywhere between a few minutes to a half-hour. If it takes longer, the knob is probably missing the initial screw.

The novice should also be aware that The Vessel must be well greased at all times. And when it comes to grease, all gourmets make their own. Store-bought grease is considered tacky. Still, there is that rare pot that has a history of turning out a crusty hasty pudding instead of one that crumbles when the proper time comes. For this rare Vessel a no-stick coating might be called for. Choose a coating that works for your particular pot. You'll know the right one when things don't get partially cooked and stick to the pan. As for pot placement: In gourmet cooking, Vessel placement varies. A four-star multiorgasmic recipe will designate, with a minimum of fuss and delay, the proper placement for a Vessel.

Now, let's get down to It and learn how the great orgasmic gourmets from around the world went about achieving the multiorgasmic delight.

Did a gourmet cook up the first vaginal orgasm? Nope, science claims the orgasmic delight was passed down to human females from the animal world. If females in the insect or fish world have experienced the delight of a Big "O," God only knows. Indeed, we can only hope the birds and bees have tumbled for an "O." In humans, the earliest recorded recipes for multiorgasmic delight were the meaty entrées cooked up in ancient India, somewhere in the time span of A.D. 100 to 500. These formulas were gathered into one spicy tome, the *Kama Sutra*, and geared to delight the senses of males and females dedicated to experiencing the full-bodied flavor of pungent sex. Credit for the spiciest part—sixty-four exotic menus for experiencing an orgasmic delight—goes to the sage (wise guy, not the herb) Vatsyanna Mallanage. And, while it is true that most of Vatsyanna's recipes were formulas that concentrated on the one-shot ambrosia of a male's orgasm, this sage was the first to appreciate, and record, the capacity of The Vessel for making more orgasmic delights than you could shake a stick at.

Positioning The Vessel, to achieve multiboiling points, is paramount in the recipes of the *Kama Sutra*. Many gourmets find these strategic placements for The Vessel—combined with tail-spinning aerobatics—read more like recipes for a crackpot. Take the recipe called the "Spinning Top," where The Vessel sits upside down with its mouth turned to receive the tool for stirring. To achieve a boiling point, The Vessel is required to spin like a dervish around the tool to generate the heat necessary for creating a vaginal orgasmic delight. For the laid-back gourmets that predominate in the Western world, Vatsyanna's recipes have been appraised in the main as half-baked concoctions.

Far more popular in the West are the nutritious multiorgasmic recipes that peaked in China during the seventh century. Since, supposedly, meat is in short supply in the Orient (and, *supposedly*, a little meat goes a long way), gourmets in the East concentrated on fishy recipes that required a healthy dose of cream from a bubbling pot, one capable of bubbling over and over, again and again.

What is even more intriguing about these fishy recipes to health nuts in the West is the Chinese claim that these multiorgasmic recipes cure or prevent "The One Hundred Ailments." Not only that—the more boiling points a Vessel achieves, the more robust and hearty the fish in the pot will get. Now in the West, this is not considered a crock-of-shit. Especially in the health-conscious United States, where everyone is determined to live it up forever and will get muscle-bound—to the peak of their pointed heads—to prove it.

Not a bad point actually. For when it comes down to

stirring in these Oriental multiorgasmic recipes, they, indeed, call for a hardy soul. Take the recipe called the "Tiger's Tread," which requires a master chef to do all of his stirring on his knees, while his tool—a leakproof instrument—penetrates deeply all the pot's innards.

Note: Westerners will find that most of the Oriental multiorgasmic recipes call for a leakproof instrument. Another Note: And most Westerners might find this a difficult—if not impossible—tool to come by.

The "Tiger's Tread" then calls for the tool to give The Vessel five shallow love stirs, followed by eight deep ones. After several sets of five to eights, the chef, with mounting excitement, will know he has pulled this recipe off when the pot's innards—rhythmically contracting and expanding as the heat gets more and more intense—comes to a seething, satisfying boil.

One boil cures one ailment. There are ninety-nine more to go! They are heavenly recipes—if the chef lives through It.

Also, the novice researching these Oriental recipes should be aware there is an art to stirring in the East. A tool is never simply plunged in a pot and banged around from side to side. The best example for maneuvering a tool to create a vaginal orgasmic delight is described—with great delicacy—by the Taoist master Tung in "Nine Styles of Moving the Jade Stalk." It should go without saying these movements are reserved for stirring inside the "female crucible," not for waving in the wind.

> The Jade Stalk, first, is flailed from the right to the left, in the same way that a brave warrior breaks up the ranks of the enemy; second, the Stalk moves up and down, like a wild horse bucking through a swiftly running stream; third it dives in and pulls out, like a flight of sea gulls playing in the waves; fourth, it alternates deep and shallow love strokes, swiftly, like the sparrow

diving for the grains of rice that have been left in the mortar; fifth by making a deep stroke that plunges like a large stone when it is thrown into the sea; sixth, it pushes in slowly, like a snake entering its hole; seventh, it rushes in swiftly, like a frightened rat rushes into his home; eighth, slowly it moves, like a hawk grabbing for an elusive rabbit; and ninth, the best of all, it rises up and plunges down, like a boat with a full sail as it braves a heavy gale.

In a somewhat more realistic style, Tung winds up these rules for stirring in a crucible with:

Deep and shallow, slow and quick, straight and slanting all these are to be known by their own special characteristics. . . . One should apply each at the proper time, with a joyous spontaneity, rather than clinging to a single style that suits only personal idiosyncrasies.

Obviously, gourmets that get a charge out of using an automatic blender can pull the plug when it comes to whipping up an Oriental delight.

Gourmets in the East also had a variety of names for the fluids that bubble away in the "female crucible." They sound more than appetizing, as well they should. For a sampling: "Moon Flower Waters," "Love Juice," "Lotus-nectar," "Moon fluid," "Essence of Woman," "Peak Medicine," "Moon Flower Medicine," and "White Metal."

The Vessel is also given a few appetizing nicknames in these Oriental recipes. Now, who wouldn't want to take a sip from a Vessel called: "The White Tiger's Cavern," or "The Purple Mushroom Peak," or "The Mysterious Gate," or better yet, "The Palace of Yin?"

As to how multiorgasmic delights become health foods—it's very simple. If the stirring tool never leaks into the pot but, instead, slurps up the pot's juices when it reaches a climax, the purity of this heavenly juice becomes a

Fountain of Youth for a sucker. Of course "mutual absorption" is sometimes recommended in the East. But, ideally, a tool should leak—*after absorbing!*—in only two (tops three) out of ten recipe makings.

This is not an easy recipe for gourmets in the West to come down to making. Mutual-absorption recipes abound in the West, where tools leak more often than not and pots have been calibrated to climax when they do. Ideally, that's the way to make it in the West.

Before we move on to sample the recipes concocted in the Western world, a health nut should nose out the menus for orgasmic delights that were plotted out in *The Perfumed Garden*. The recipes are Arabic and they date back to the fifteenth century. They are also, pointedly, health-oriented. For example, this book warns that dipping into sexual intercourse on an empty stomach has a tendency to weaken the eyesight. Even more precarious is dipping into a course on a full stomach, when the chances increase for rupturing the intestines. And, worst of all, a course shared with an old woman acts like a fatal poison.

Female gourmets who twitch at the very mention of an orgasmic delight would be wise to turn up their noses when it comes to recipes in *The Perfumed Garden*. One sniff of this formula will prove it:

> It is said that there are women of great experience who, lying with a man, elevate one of their feet vertically in the air, and upon that foot a lamp is set full of oil, and with the wick burning. While the man is ramming [their Vessel], they keep the lamp steady and burning, and the oil is not spilled. Their coition is not impeded by this exhibition, but it must require great previous practice on the part of both.

Both??? Even for one, this formula has a decided fishy smell.

Moving Westward. As the sun sinks in the West, so goes

It and the glories of vaginal orgasmic delights. This was especially true from the late eighteenth century until well into the twentieth in many European countries and the Americas. The cause for this decline in appetite for vaginal delights is due to recipes taking on a decided medicinal flavor after science poked its nose into the pot. Medical science decided that it was time to turn down the heat on boiling pots. Some scientists even went so far as to recommend putting The Vessel in a cooler before it got too hot to handle. Those were soggy days indeed for whipping up a vaginal delight (note the singular—multiorgasms were thought impossible to make in those times). Naturally, as Vessels began to dry up, leakproof stirring instruments became petrified and wooden.

Hand-me-down recipes became the thing of the day when It came down to orgasmic delights. Even the days of cooking up a delight in a double boiler were considered behinds that were behind the times. The question is: Why did these nations, that once gloried in creating orgasmic delights, and the more the merrier, let medical science prescribe for the pot?

Science, somewhat late in the game, discovered that the Crud, syphilis, was all over the place causing blindness, insanity, heart disease, the disfigurement of a leper, and finally, for many, an agonizing, protracted death. Where was the Crud? In more European military tools and in their Vessels than you could shake an army of sticks at.

Pots stopped whistling a merry tune. Stirring tools were stuffed, posthaste, into baggy sleeves called condoms. Those who sneered at these tacky sleeves passed the scum of devastating Crud over most of Europe, which floated eventually overseas. It was a most unappetizing time. Unappetizing, but far from a starvation diet.

For, unsavory as it might seem, this deadly contaminant—at a minimum, noxious enough to make flesh rot on the bone—could not curb the thousands who still craved for vaginal orgasmic delights. Proof of the pudding, with Crud all over the world, orgasmic recipe books were published in the West during the late eighteenth and early nineteenth centuries. A first. Granted, most were private publications, but, bet your spice box, all were composed by master chefs. It took another century, the twentieth, before a female gourmet got her recipes slid under the covers of a book by Anon. A tidy first.

Two master chefs wrote not only books—they wrote volumes; both totally different, and why not when they had decidedly opposite tastes and appetites. We're looking at the Marquis de Sade and Casanova.

The Marquis, admittedly not a gourmet for everyone's taste, did not have his recipes published until the end of the eighteenth century (he began writing them in 1777). As for that tasteful gourmet, Casanova, he began his recipe countdown—which in the end totaled twelve stirring volumes—in 1789 and was not published until the nineteenth century. But, then, one can never count on taste when it comes down to orgasmic delights.

Since de Sade's recipes tend to lean on sour grapes and whipping rather than stirring the pot, a budding gourmet is advised to give these recipes a pass—especially if one is interested in making vaginal multiorgasmic delights. Far better at savoring each morsel are the recipes passed down by Casanova, a connoisseur of thousands of orgasmic delights. For example, here is a stirring statistic: This fourteen-star gourmet, Casanova, brought a Vessel to fourteen separate, delicious boiling points just with the stirring from his—one erect—firm tool. It was never a pinch of this and pinch of that when it came to potluck for Casanova.

It has been estimated Casanova stirred up vaginal orgasmic delights for some thirty-five years. And the secret for his success as a world-renowned gourmet appears to be that the great lover was a flaming romantic. Proof for this lies in the computed results tabulated in *The Intimate Sex Lives of Famous People*. The authors of this book assigned seven trained researchers "to comb the 12 volumes of Casanova's *History of My Life*." They were surprised to find: "Casanova had a tenth of the number of sex partners claimed by Sarah Bernhardt, Guy de Maupassant, Elvis Presley, Ninon de Lenclos [all over a thousand, except for Guy, who has a record in the thousands], and others. It became clear to us that Casanova was not interested in being the world's busiest lover. He was interested in the quality of each encounter [132 plus], in savoring each morsel."

As a vaginal gourmet, Casanova enjoyed savoring each morsel from a broad spread of comestibles. He stirred pots that varied in age from eleven to over fifty. The Venetian lover shook pots from every European country and even expanded to one African. He had a preference for turning on the heat for servant girls and wealthy gentlewomen. He was also at the bottom of churning, to a satisfying pitch, the Vessels of two nuns after they—with faith, hope, and charity—took into the fold his amorous tool. His implement is also pinpointed for breaking in thirty-one virgin Vessels. The minimum stirring time is recorded at a palatable speed of fifteen minutes; the longest, seven—what's your pleasure?— hours.

Casanova's tool was not leakproof. For example; in one twenty-four-hour period, he creamed one pot twelve separate times. The secret was that he had a built-in timer, so perfect, it took the guesswork out of when that delicate moment came to add a touch of cream to the pot.

But his tool wasn't perfect. Casanova admits to three premature ejaculations and seven, down-to-earth, timeworn times he was unable to lift his tool for stirring. He preferred stirring the pot to licking it. Guzzling and gobbling were fast-refreshment operations and tasteless substitutes for this great lover of stirring, and stirring, and stirring the pot.

Moving further West, to England, and a century back, there is a word portrait worth quoting that decribes the capability of a Vessel to come to manifold boiling points. This tail-spinning description, painted by a maid billed as Cuntilla, appears in a late-seventeeth-century play entitled *Sodom or the Quintessence of Debauchery.*

> *Here is a mine or ocean full of treasure,*
> *'tis we alone enjoy the chiefest pleasure*
> *Whilst men do toil and moil to spend their strength,*
> *The pleasure does to us rebound at length.*
> *Men when they've spent are like some piece of wood*
> *Or an insipid thing, tho flesh and blood,*
> *While we are still desirous of more*
> *And valiantly dare challenge half a score,*
> *Nay canthes like we'll swive with forty men;*
> *Then home to our husbands and there swive again.*

The author of this play, which is attributed to John Wilmot, the Earl of Rochester, gave all the female characters up-front place-names such as: Cuntigratia, Swivia, Fuckadilla, Clytoris, Cunticula, and Officina. But don't look to this play for recipes for vaginal delights, since this literary work is devoted to the manly art of buggery. Personally, the Earl had a bisexual appetite. But, unappetizing to say, in his poems, the Earl made the vagina as unsavory as a can of contaminated worms. Here's a tasteless example:

> *I send for my whore, when for fear of a Clap*
> *I fuck in her hand, and spew in her Lap;*
> *. . . Then slily she leaves me, and t'revenge the Affront*
> *At once she bereaves me of Money and Cunt.*
> *If by Chance then I wake, hot-headed and drunk*
> *What a Coil do I make for the Loss of my Punk?*

I storm, and I roar, and I fall in a Rage,
And missing my Whore, I bugger my Page.
Then Crop-sick all Morning, I rail at my Men,
And in Bed I lie yawning 'till Eleven again.

Two centuries later, in the late nineteenth, an English Casanova semisurfaced. Semi because to this day he remains anonymous. Mr. Anon took 11 volumes (each of which totaled 385 pages—or a smashing 4,235) to write his recipe-book delights, one volume less than Casnova's. But, if a tabulation were ever made of Anon's sexual partners, there is no doubt his total would plunge way, way ahead of his Italian counterpart; perhaps because sexual variety was the spice of life to this Victorian gent.

Whatever the amount totals up, there is never a doubt when one reads his recipe book (reduced today, sad to say, to one volume entitled *My Secret Life*) that no one, who's ever stirred on this globe, has ever had a greater appreciation—in truth, an addiction—for vaginal orgasmic delights than Mr. Anon. Or for female genitals, period or no period. Here is just one melting description of his crush on the female genital area:

> She was exquisitely formed, plump to perfection, without an ounce too much fat, and had the loveliest little cunt I ever saw, with a little nutty shaped clitoris, with a mere line of inner lip, and delicately puffed lips covered with bright, chestnut colored, silky, yet crisp hair, which only just covered her mount, and stopped half way down between the bum hole. Her flesh enervated me with its sweet smell, she was one of those delicious-smelling women. . . . I could not wait to enjoy my eyesight. . . .

As a gourmet of vaginal orgasmic delights, Mr. Anon was receptive to pitching in and relishing the subtleties of manifold pots. Naturally, there were some he found more appetizing than others. Here is a rare hairsplitting example:

> When on the bed I looked at her hidden beauties, and found such a cunt as I never saw before or since. — About every five years or so I think I have had women whose cunts were very uncommon in some particular.
> This Saxon's sexual trough had roly poly lips, with lots of thick bush which covered her mount, but not high up. The hair on the lips thinned as usual until their junction with her thighs where it began immediately to reappear, and thickened down about three or four inches forming little beards on each side of her cunt. . . . and the tufts reminded me of goats' beards.

He goes on to say this Saxon maid was quite proud of her hairy appendages that, personally, he found—though tantalizingly unique—not quite up his alley.

The English Casanova, in a comparison study, found each vessel was unique—well almost. Take this nosy analysis:

> Out of a hundred cunts, not one is quite like to another, there is always some difference noticible [sic] in them. —In my belief, there is as much difference in the look of cunts as there is in noses. —But sisters' cunts I think are generally somewhat alike.

Note the "generally."

This astute observer of female genitals also came up with this in-depth comparison:

> I believe there never was a prick so big in any way that a cunt could not take it without pain, and even pleasurably. Its tip might perhaps knock at the portals of the womb too hard for some, but that is all. I have heard women say that the harder those knocks were the more pleasure it gave them. All the talk I have heard of

pricks being so large that women could not, or would not, take them up them is sheer nonsense. Several women have told me so. Some said that they love to see and handle big ones. None said that such stretches gave them more physical pleasure than those of moderate size. The elasticity and receptivity of a cunt is in fact as wonderful as its constrictive power. The small prick of a boy thirteen it will tighten round and exhaust, as well as one as big as the spoke of a cartwheel, and it will give pleasure to both equally.

For those who find Anon's recipes a bit gamy, especially in a feast exploring the glories of vaginal delights, let us take a page from twentieth-century fiction; the poetic recipe prescribed by author D. H. Lawrence for his heroine, the sex-starved Lady Chatterley:

> Then as he began to move, in the sudden helpless orgasm [his], there awoke in her new strange trills rippling inside her. Rippling, rippling, like a flapping overlapping of soft flames, soft as feathers, running to points of brilliance, exquisite, exquisite and melting her all molten inside. It was like bells rippling up and up to a culmination. She lay unconscious of the wild little cries she uttered to the last. But it was over too soon, too soon. . . .

Ah! But was Lady Chatterley's lover finished stirring? Hardly!

> . . . and he never quite slipped from her, and she felt the soft bud of him within her stirring, and strange rhythms flushing up into her with a strange rhythmic growing motion, swelling and swelling till it filled all her cleaving consciousness, and then began again the unspeakable motion that was not really motion, but pure deepening whirlpools of sensation swirling deeper and deeper through all her tissue and consciousness, till she

was one perfect concentric fluid of feeling, and she lay there crying in unconscious inarticulate cries. The voice out of the uttermost night, the life!

In literature the longest, and the driest, description for concocting a vaginal orgasmic delight took thirty yawning pages. It threw in everything but the kitchen sink and had the thrill of bubbles created by a can of Drāno. Written in the same era as Lawrence's spine-tingling recipe, it was, with little doubt, the harbinger of therapeutic orgasmic deliriums. This orgasmic deliverance was a hallucination concocted by a long-winded Irishman named James Joyce. It leaked—all over the place—in his macho tome *Ulysses*. Translators (from English to English) tell us Molly Bloom has reached an orgasmic peak in the final phrase on the final page of this incoherent masterpiece. Molly percolates to orgasm, seemingly on her lonesome, after being stirred by thirty pages of wallowing in a stream of consciousness and a smattering of raunchy words. Molly's pot must have been, *indeed*, hard up.

Even the U.S. judge who dropped the fifteen-year obscenity ban on *Ulysses* entering the United States had these findings to report: ". . . that in reading *Ulysses* in its entirety . . . did not excite sexual impulses or lustful thoughts but that its net effect on them [two of his pals] was only that of a somewhat tragic and powerful commentary on the inner lives of men and women."

And that is just a taste of what's to come when it comes down to writing down the recipe for vaginal orgasmic delights.

Today in the United States and other areas of the world, more women than ever before are writing vaginal orgasmic recipe books. These books are the basis for healthy recipes with exotic and erotic flavoring. Here's to one orgasm, two orgasms, three orgasms, more!

7

LOCK, STOCK, AND BARREL—A TITLE SEARCH OF VAGINAL ESTATES

Virginity and chastity are going down the tubes. They are being liquidated by owner/operators of vaginal estates who have opted to swill The Pill. This entitlement—sexual enjoyment minus the lien of pregnancy—has increased the personal property value of vaginal estates for millions of owner/operators.

For a comparable low interest rate in virginity, one would have to look back to primitive times. (As for chastity, it was a pointless endeavor not known from Adam.) In those pagan-god-fearing days, virgins were sacrificed—along with other goats, et cetera—in hope a benevolent god would increase flocks and crops. From this pagan perspective, one might assume a virginal vagina was a V.I.P.; that is, Very Important Piece. Wrong. When we get to the bottom of it, it was the prolific, productive vagina that was pegged *the* V.I.P.

Benevolent gods were chancy. But the vagina churning out, year in year out, mankind's most needed tool—kids to maintain the crops and flocks—really delivered. The vagina had an unseen mystical power. It became top god.

It was a sexually naïve world. Mankind believed the vagina chugged away producing babes on its lonesome. With this singular creative power, it figures the fertile vagina would be crowned a living, life-giving god. Humans were a long piece down the primitive road before he/she grasped that the penis had its stake in the output of the vagina; theirs was a naïve world that some virgins—yes, there are still a few out there—live in to this day.

Nailing the penis' stake in vaginal productivity is credited to early shepherds who computed an increase in their flocks after ewes took a heated interest in physical abutments with an available ram. Separate ram from ewe in heat—no increase. Previous to this penetrating tabulation, the base investment a human male made on a vaginal site was a drop in the bucket. That his liquid investment—semen—was one source for pouring future foundations—heirs—did not sink in till modern times.

Squatters' Rights

Once man appraised his stake as *the* pipeline for creation of a future work force, the vagina was reevaluated. V.I.P. for the vagina now translated Vaginal Industrial Park. As might be expected, the penis was now top god. And a popular one—you could visualize this god, make images and symbols that all could recognize. The dark mystery of the

vagina was kaput. The inflated, bigger-is-better, penis image
was IT.

Under reevaluation, the vagina slid from god to a piece
of property—an Industrial Park stuck with sticky stockholders. Loss of status as top god was not the worst of it.
Vaginal operators were facing squatter's rights. Gone was
their option to the right of joint tenancy. Males were out to
stake their claims—her vagina could be taken over as his
private property. Legit vaginal entrepreneurship was a thing
of the past.

Blanket Mortgaging

With sticky stockholders now in control, vaginal operators faced a period of economic adjustment, better known
as deep economic recession. This financial imbalance originated when man moved out from primitive isolation into
village life. A tribal society could afford to share; in village
living each man had to look out for his own. Personal property—land, crops, flocks—brought the weight of rightful
heirs. Since the secret to a rightful heir was stashed in the
vagina, man invented a manly contract—namely, marriage.
And with marriage came a crown—"head of the family"—
that deeded him air rights, tunnel rights, and all laying between, over his contracted vaginal property. Needless to
add, under this deed, the head of the family also laid as
much pipe as he could come up with.

And needless to add, under the contract of marriage, a
vaginal operator was buried in blanket mortgaging under
the lien of inflated reproduction costs. The major output a
wife faced was popping rightful heirs. Pop a questionable
one and she was out on her tail. If she produced no heirs, it
was the same sad tale.

Sexual Variance in Society and History cites an ancient
Egyptian exception for production of heirs outside the marriage contract—but for adultery there were no exceptions.

Rescind that; there was one exception—for adultery—the head of the family:

> The laws made a clear distinction between a concubine and a wife, and a bachelor could technically keep a concubine without being married. Adultery by a woman was cause for divorce and could be punished by burning at the stake, but a married male was permitted other sexual partners. A husband could divorce a wife more or less at his convenience, provided he paid her compensation, but no such freedom was given a woman. If a couple failed to have children, they could jointly acquire a young female slave to act as a sexual proxy for the wife, and any children she bore would be legitimated and emancipated at the husband's death.

Wife or concubine, vaginal output for the head of the family in ancient times faced constant assessed valuation—especially in cases of absentee landlords—for no owner of vaginal property had to abide by a bond that made him "alien to his roots." If a son of a bitch showed up in his domain, the vaginal operator was nailed with immediate eviction proceedings.

Vaginal operators were facing hard times. In addition to blanket mortgaging, partial foreclosure, and the burden of inflated costs, they faced threats of demolition under a cloud of title deeded Adultery. Condemnation by the head of the family, nailing up a sign ADULTERESS, was all that was needed for devaluation, dispossession, and possible demolition as a tenement holder/operator.

Isolated into powerless plots and blanketed with binder clauses, operators of vaginal property adjusted to the title holding of servient estates.

Encroachment Proceedings

But there were, in ancient times, unique societies where depreciation of vaginal properties was marginal. In one society, there was a decided appreciation—that is, the ancient Hebrews, who decreed a husband must give his wife sexual satisfaction and do it on her command. This clause in the marriage contract must have kept a well-heeled sport hopping, since under Hebrew law a husband was allowed as many wives as he could support—financially. That a Hebrew husband was also allowed as many concubines as he could support brought no sexual sweat since these slaves could make no demands.

Over these poky centuries, there were operators of vaginal estates who put up a battle to retain personal management rights. Many of these independents sold their vaginal property as they saw fit. Marketing their vaginal property meant survival for those not under contract of marriage or sold as concubines for sexual slavery. Among these independents, some nailed adulteress, were vaginal operators who fought to get a fair shake—to bring an end to encroachment proceedings deeded by marriage or slavery, and a fair appraisal for all vaginal estates. Survivalist or freedom fighter, all independent operators were condemned as whores.

Independents fought a losing battle against holders of conventional mortgages, the head of the family. In the end their closing costs for these battles wound up as devastating—if not killing—penalties.

Take the private sector, where independent operators were slapped with fines and eviction notices. Independents were publicly stoned or had their hair torn out by owners and their own—operators of vaginal estates—as symbols of their crime. Far worse were the penalties where the fee by law was absolute. Under law, independents faced a branding for life penalized by: chopping off a nose, slicing off an ear, or/and gouging out an eye (rarely both eyes, as they were to see, for a lifetime, the punishment for *their* heinous crime). Less obvious, totally torturous, independents were sexually desensitized via penalty of legal dismemberment: the chopping off of a clitoris, whacking off their breasts, attaching crude locks and chains to the vulva, or/and a burning stake shoved into their tiny vaginal estate till there was nothing left but a barren hole.

Vaginal operators, who favored these penalties for independents, faced penalties of their own, though often not recognized. In the West, they were imprisoned in home sweet home. In the East, many were imprisoned in harems. Either side of the globe, many learned to love, even adore their jailer, the head of the family.

Stupid? Why ever not? With few exceptions (upper-class women in Egypt, Sparta, and Rome), education was nonexistent, so were monies and property holding. Social activities outside the home were taboo. Social activities inside the home were child rearing; cooking or overseer for a cook; sewing till you dropped dead; and sexual availability till your vagina was a dried-up old prune.

But, hold your tears, the vagina was about to be saved—well, redeemed. That the penis was also to be saved is another redeeming tale. Well, almost.

Redemption Proceedings

If vaginal operators thought they had to keep their end up and take it while lying down under control of the head of the family, they would learn, under decree by theologians for the early church, there was the devil to pay.

Around 600 B.C., a religion in Persia (now called Iran) initiated the domino effect that hundreds of centuries later would take over, in the Western world and areas of the Middle East, management control of vaginal properties from heads of families. This takeover took well into A.D. to entrench its authority.

Zoroaster, founder of the Persian idealistic religion Zoroastrianism, was out to whip the gods into shape. From primitive times till Zoro came on the scene, man conceived gods with good and bad qualities—a humanistic approach. Too human for Zoro. Bad gods, by their example, inflamed the senses. Good gods should have no senses. To lead the good life, man—and woman—would emulate good gods and drop their senses. The nonsense of fasting and celibacy were Zoro's solutions to rid mankind of evil. In his hedonistic world, Zoro was whipping a dead horse.

For the next 200 centuries Zoro's nonsensical ideals were shelved. Then an idealistic group of Greek philosophers borrowed Zoro's nonsense to create and promote their ideal—a Platonic society, a spiritual world devoid of sensual feeling and the gratification of desire. Like Zoro, these non-sense philosophers first took a whip to sensual gods. After shaping up gods, they got ballsy and took after man.

A Platonic prospectus—elimination of a balloon clause that kept the head of the family pumping away in Vaginal Industrial Parks—was appraised by laymen as out of this world when it came down to reproduction losses. But the Platonist right of way to call it as they saw it was never questioned in the free society adopted by the ancient Greeks. So males, exposed to the teachings of the idealistic phi-losophers, nodded in profound agreement and then went their lusty way—screwing wanton gals or boys and, often, their two-tongued philosophers.

Ah, but what about those few females exposed to these Platonic ideals? For those, whose vaginas were encumbered by blanket mortgaging and the debit but no credit for the bounty pregnancy, elimination of a balloon clause in their vaginal estates had the ring of a fair contract, but not for those independent operators who, restricted to the upper classes of Greece's free society, maintained a right of control over their vaginal estates. Elimination of the balloon clause in their vaginal estates meant devaluation and loss of inter-est rate, not to mention deflation and imminent foreclosure.

Not to worry, ancient Greece was hedonistic to the hilt. Under their lenient codes for those plugged into AC/DC, the balloon clause hung in there—there being either vaginal or anal estates. So, down the tubes went the nonsense ideals of the aesthetic Greek philosophers.

DEPRECIATION AND FORECLOSURE

As the decadent society of Rome crumbled, founders of early Christianity began a search for moral foundations to build an antihedonistic world. They zeroed in on the bottom line—management control of genital areas via the nonsensual, aesthetic principles of Zoroastrianism and Platonism.

The early Christians were out to become an almighty powerhouse. For total power, they had to usurp control of vaginal properties held for hundreds of centuries by the heads of families. And since the whole caboodle were a pack of heathens their conscience was clear—better than clear, it was down right pure.

And that's when theologians for the early church came up with a fail-safe, brilliant plot. Make virtue paramount to marriage. With this as a heavenly foundation, the church became the "true" head of the family. Man, you are looking at a whole new ball game! Down came a judgement on genital areas: Sex was serious sin, except for procreation (mind you sir, not propagation of a name or a line) to maintain a Christian world. The Church decreed it was no longer "normal" for all God's chosen ones to marry, since a celibate was a perfect representative—and servant—for a nonsexual deity. As for the noncelibate (married or damned): His/her duty was to function, first, within the ideals laid down by the Church; second, within the rules of the community; and, last and least, within the influence experienced in family existence.

Gone, except in Scripture, was the admonition from

99

Genesis when God tells Eve, "In sorrow thou shalt bring forth children, and thy desire shall be to thy husband, and he shall rule over thee."

Indeed the vagina was under new management. As for the new controllers, they did a hell of a job. Sex was evil—a benchmark for the Devil. Procreation was under a warranty deeded by the church. And to insure conversion from the holders of private vaginal properties, early theologians started listing vaginal estates under sewer system. You better believe it, what we're looking at is *the pits*.

Proof: Take the appraisal of Tertullian, a most influential third-century theologian, describing woman as "a temple built on a sewer." For a follow-up, his damning appraisal of Eve the church's first lady:

> Do you realize, Eve, that it is you? The curse God pronounced on your sex weighs still in the world. Guilty, you must bear its hardships. You are the devil's gateway, you desecrated the fatal tree, you first betrayed the law of God, you softened up with your cajoling words the man against whom the devil could not prevail by force. The image of God, Adam, you broke him as if he were a plaything. *You* deserved death, and it was the son of God who had to die!

To be sure, Eve had had her unfair share of knocks as a bad plot before Tertullian and the third century. Take the damning citation in Genesis where Eve was slapped with: the cause of man's downfall; a temptress that brought upon the destruction of Paradise; and, the basis for God's damning the snake to scoot on its belly till eternity.

Damning citations slapped on vaginal estates by the early theologians sank to an all-time low. Looking back, you had to hand it to them though for certain damn creative ideas when it came to assessing their evaluation of the vaginal sites of both Eve and the Virgin Mary.

Take the early theologian John, "the Golden Mouth" who came up with this nugget claiming Adam and Eve had indeed done it in Eden, *otherwise* God would have made Adam's companion a man instead of a woman; and the sex these two virgins participated in had nothing to do with making babes—that creation they invented after the Fall. Since nugget head's theory bypassed the obvious connection that Adam could do it in Paradise with a male companion, what we're looking at is his base assessment that the vaginal site was a disgraceful plant—a sewer plant.

Damning the vaginal passage with its reproductive system for input and output as a sewer system brought the early theologians to a unique transfer of property—that of the vaginal site for the Virgin Mary. It took some doing but finally they came up with a bill of sale selling this unique site as a one-way street going *out*. And that unique thoroughfare was constructed for one *out*. What remains a mystery to this day was who paved the way in this unique one-way passage, and how did who pull it off?

Here is a creative conception from theologian Justin Martyr, a saint if there ever was one. Justin said no way could the mother of God possibly conceive His son through an act of lust and defilement invented by Eve, the scourge of all mankind. Mary, Justin assessed, was a virgin and by the grace of God conceived without lowering herself to the sinful act. From that date on, Mary was not only a virgin, she was a blessed blooming eunuch.

For a concept that performed a transexual operation, we should examine this one recorded by Thomas in the Gnostic Gospel:

> Simon Peter said to them, "Let Mary go forth among us, for women are not worthy of the life." Jesus said, "See, I will lead her that I might make her a male, so that she may become a living spirit like you males. For every

woman who makes herself a male shall enter the kingdom of heaven."

It is no mystery that this one-sex Gnostic sect petered out in no time.

But the concept of the Virgin Mary's singular conception remains, for some, a mystery to this day. How was *It* done? *Alone of All Her Sex: The Myth and the Cult of the Virgin Mary* lists some penetrating hints handed down in Scripture:

> The operation of God on the virginal womb of Mary was prefigured in Scripture in a score of different ways: she was fecundated, like the fleece of Gideon drenched with dew while all around remained dry (Judges 6:36–40); the rod of Aaron, like the womb of the Virgin, flowered of its own accord (Numbers 17:8); the stone in the dream of Nebuchadnezzar "was cut of the mountain with no hands" (Daniel 2:34); the staff of Moses turned spontaneously into a serpent (Exodus 7:9); the manna fell like rain, a free gift from heaven (Exodus 16:14); the unaccompanied finger of God wrote the tablets of the law (Deuteronomy 9:10).

If all these hints indicate that the early theologians had yet to get Mary's act together, you're on top of it. Finally, in A.D. 390, Pope Siricius came flat out proclaiming Mary "an inviolate virgin during pregnancy and the birth of Christ." From that time on, everyone had to agree: Mary was different— period or no period.

This proclamation, from the supreme authoritarian for the church, left women with "ordinary" passages for input and output in a hell of a hole.

SEWERAGE IN A SEWER SYSTEM

In the fifth century, a former broad jumper, Augustine, took a major leap and landed on Chastity. Brushing himself off from the filth of broad jumping, he decided to rake vaginas over the coals. For two centuries theologians had been searching for the origin of evil. With a poisonous pen, Augustine, now a recorder of deeds as a theologian, documented the Origin of Evil under an abstract of title he called Concupiscence.

According to Augustine, sin originated in the Garden of Eden when Eve, tempting Adam with sensuous desire, got the ball rolling to commit the first evil act. This act doomed mankind, unless man achieved personal salvation, since all humans were born into our world contaminated by concupiscence—the Original Sin.

Augustine, in passing on, suggested the male organ might be the transmitter of this hereditary taint, but this could occur only if a male's pure organ submitted to sexual embrace. This damning definition of Original Sin, which exists to this day, made both the womb and its entrance, the vagina, the basic source for all evil committed on this earth.

Down through time, the vaginal zone had been subdivided under a variety of titles by macho developers, but none so depreciating as Augustine's. For example Hymen (a thin membrane that partially covers—in supposed virgins—the entrance to the vagina) was the Greek god of marriage. An intact hymen was considered proof of virginity. A teensy tissue of red tape in most marriage contracts—a lien the penis knew not from. God save Hymen; he knew where it was at.

Conversion of a virginal estate to a nonvirginal one, from the perspective of depreciation or appreciation, can be traced through the origin of other macho terms. Check out sex. Its origin traces back to *secare*, a Roman verb that means to cut or sever. Or *chastity*, a term originating from *castus*, a Latin term, which in the feminine gender, means conforming to religious rules and rites. Do a double check on virgin, which originates from *virgo*, and in Latin translates, a human female not yet "known" by man. Closer in time,

Webster suggests *virgo* in Latin means "a supple and flexible branch."

In *The Second Sex*, feminist author Simone de Beauvoir traces this legend of a medieval knight down to one.

> ... who pushed his way with difficulty through thorny bushes to pick a rose of hitherto unbreathed fragrance; he not only found it but broke the stem, and it was then that he made it his own. The image is so clear that in popular language to "take her flower" from a woman means to destroy her virginity; and this expression, of course, has given origin to the word "defloration."

In the 1982 edition of *Slang and Euphemism*, synonyms under *deflower* are listed as:

Break	Perforate
Cop a bean	Pick her cherry
Cop a cherry	Pluck
Crack a Judy's teacup	Punch
Crack a pitcher	Puncture
Defloration	Ransack
Devirginate	Ruin
Devirginize	Scuttle
Dock	Trim
Double-event	Trim the buff
Ease	Violate
Get through	

That the flower of virginity has its season is also pointed out in *The Second Sex* when de Beauvoir relates the rot of a seedy conversation overheard between a woman remarking to a male about the beauty of a lady who [now a bit long in the tooth], surprisingly, was still a virgin; and the male's put-down: "But think of all the cobwebs inside."

Before the rosy appreciation for vaginal estates that evolved during medieval time, the perspective was far from rosy in the pits of the Dark Ages. What we're looking at is bedrock for vaginal property in the West. From prehistoric times the vagina had gone from an idolized piece, to a piece of industry, to a hole-in-the-wall substitute for Paradise, to the pits—a sewer plant leaking evil for all mankind.

As demolition, it was smashing. It took seven centuries, after Augustine nailed the vagina as a pit of all evil, before a redeveloper appeared. Bet titties it was a woman.

THE POWER OF EMINENT DOMAIN

Eleanor of Aquitaine was the ideal champ for redevelopment of ruined vaginal estates. First, she had power—queen of France *and* England; next, loaded—an heiress with the clout of her own dough; and, from a vaginal perspective, a sense for romance that changed Western history. Not to mention, a royal belly full of input for output of her vaginal estate.

As Vaginal Industrial Parks, queens, either West or East, were well aware of the chain of title. Under two regal husbands, Eleanor was pressed into service turning out heirs for their thrones. First time around, as queen for Louis VII of France, Eleanor turned out two daughters—but no heirs (sons). In France, it was grounds for annulment if a queen did not turn out royal heirs. But Louis adored his beauteous, capricious queen, *until* Eleanor went on a Crusade. As adored wife and a royal Vaginal Industrial Park, Eleanor accompanied Louis on the Second Crusade. It was during those years Eleanor investigated the appreciation for vaginal estates in the East.

While Louis was busy fighting his Crusade, Eleanor was busy on a crusade of her own—the freedom of managing her vaginal estate. Eleanor had a ball. In fact several balls, for during her five years in the East she celebrated with five different lovers. The ball was over when, disenchanted, Louis took Eleanor prisoner, yanked her back to France to the boring work of trying to turn out male heirs.

Fifteen years down the pike produced nary an heir. Louis, regal to the bone, dumped Eleanor. Two months later, dumped at a ripe age of thirty, Eleanor took her sweet revenge. She married a nineteen-year-old stud, Henry Plantagenet, a ducal rival of Louie the ex, a future king of England, Normandy, and the west of France. In the next seventeen years Eleanor's Vaginal Industrial Park turned out eight babes—three daughters, five sons (two future kings of England; one of the two was the fearless warrior Richard the Lionhearted) for her king.

But Henry was no more faithful to his queen than Eleanor had been to King Louis. Revenge this time was bitter. Totally disenchanted, Eleanor was out to get Henry's crown and pop it on his heir. Henry took his revenge by banishing Eleanor to Aquitaine, a province in southwestern France that Eleanor inherited from William X, her ducal papa. That's where this disenchanting tale turns into an enchanted one. With the magic of romantic poetry and song, cherished by Eleanor since her exposure in the East, Eleanor introduced love to the West. It was a courtly introduction. A game that two could play—with just the barest hint of sexual equality.

Over the years, Eleanor was a patron of troubadours and poets, influenced by the East, who sang praises of courting a lady for her love. In chauvinistic Europe, this novel art form brought applause from ladies of the court and snickers from their lords. Wily Eleanor decided to win over the lower echelon, knights of the court. Knights were big on war games. To win their hearts, she invented a new game in which they could engage. Disguised as a game—the battle of words—Eleanor set up a love court where ladies and knights enacted mock trials for unfair practices in the

106

gamesmanship of love. Eleanor was the judge. The jury—if she allowed one—were ladies of her court.

The Natural History of Love reports the "Court of Love":

> . . . may have been a pseudo-legal hall of justice where pronouncements on love questions were seriously sought and honestly obeyed. But whether it really was this, or simply an artful way to examine a growing code of loving behavior, there is one significant fact about it: men and women met in the Court of Love on terms of mutual respect to explore the propriety, the ethics, and the aesthetics of their relationship with each other . . . a measure of profound altercation beginning to take place, at the top level of European society, in the kinds of feelings existing between the sexes.

Eleanor had only four years of playing judge in the Court of Love. Henry, always leery of his wife's facile mind and plots to grab his crown, threw Eleanor into isolation. She remained Henry's prisoner till his death fifteen years later.

But, true love never dies; the court of love was still in session. Eleanor's daughter, the Countess of Champagne (a corking title), took over the trials of losers in love. A champ at gamesmanship, the Countess soon had the knights in her court fighting for honor and love. It was a simple ploy—as judge, and jury, she often let the knights win. Here's a case report from *Tractatus:*

> A certain knight loves his lady beyond all measure and enjoyed her full embrace [Doing It?], but she did not love him with equal ardor. He sought to leave her, but she, desiring to maintain him in his former status, opposed his wish. In this affair the Countess gave this response: "It is very unseemly for a woman to seek to be loved and yet to refuse love. It is silly for anybody disrespectfully to ask of others what she herself wholly refuses to give to others."

If Eleanor wielded a magic wand to win her battle for romance, her daughter the Countess wielded a double-edged sword. That the above trial—a woman's mistreatment of a lover—was tried and sentence found in favor for a male by a *female* judge had to be, in medieval time, nonsensical play-acting—a fantasy, but a fantasy so intriguing it swept the courts of Europe.

Under redevelopment as romantic plots, vaginal properties were reevaluated. What we're seeing now is not sewer plants—we're looking at erecting model homes.

As Europe moved out from the consuming superstition of feudal isolation into the energy of the Renaissance and urban living, the bucks rolled in. With sights on material comforts, religious influence began to slide. It's the age-old story: When there's pleasure on earth, heaven can wait.

Once a unified, almighty force, in control of vaginal property, the church faced—fought and lost—insurrection under their laws for damnation and sin; that is, the chains of chastity broken after Martin Luther broke from the Roman Church and decreed celibacy and chastity were gifts from God and not self-imposed tasks.

Attachments Against Joint Tenancy

The Renaissance brought the breaking—and the making—of another chain. Married ladies moved out of the confinement of home sweet home into society. Taking a look around, they decided to redecorate—the world outside looked mighty macho. It was a slow process; most suffered the shakes after centuries of seclusion. That their vaginas, virginal or not, had been reevaluated was easy to pinpoint. All many had to do was look down and spot the padlock placed by a paranoid owner worried *now* that his vaginal property was out and about town.

From another scenario: The romantic plot, in full bloom

throughout Europe, escalated vaginal estates to treasured pieces, especially those lying in virgin territory. But treasure invites thieves, so, naturally fences with padlocks would be attached by concerned owners to their, now valuable, vaginal properites. As a prized plot, worthy of securing under the lock of enforced chastity, freedom for the vagina went from a battle of the pit to a foxy hole. But then, who promised you a rose garden?

Along with the pleasures of love imported from the East, the West imported the Eastern influence of locking up vaginal properties. In the East, security precautions for vaginal property could afford to be elaborate since their sultans bought vaginas in gross amounts and stored them in warehouses called a harem. But in the monogamous West, a harem, with its one locked-up vagina, would require a sizable investment and still smack of a dog's house.

For security more realistic—not to add logistic—center on the core of the problem and slap a padlock on the entrance to your vaginal property. (And, isn't it screwy that the device chosen to secure a vagina mimicked that organ in design and function—a hole surrounded by a protective covering waiting for the penetration of a special key.)

No one knows who invented the first chastity belt—and no one cares who invented the first padlock. All we know is the first trapped vagina surfaced in Italy during the fourteenth century. Word got about *(Women's Wear Daily?)* and it wasn't long before the straps were in vogue throughout Europe.

Design changed with the paranoia of the owner. Basically it was a steel belt, padded for the lucky ones, that encircled the waist; to this support was attached a curved plate made of sturdy metal that covered the vulva and the anus. A padlock was attached to the plate and was left to dangle between the legs. Some plates were studded with rivets—a riveting sight for a possible intruder. Some

109

sported ominous spikes—sawtoothed openings for the vulva and the anus. Whatever the design, all were inhumane, none comfortable, and all stunk—literally and figuratively—since there were only tiny openings for defecation and urination.

As a security measure, it often proved a joke since a chastity girdle was no more secure than the nearest locksmith (praise be, the contraption fell out of favor before the invention of the combination lock). That some were more secure than others often depended on the depth of an owner's paranoia about a break-in.

Here's a seamy example from eighteenth-century France. One Sieurr Pierre Berhle installed a chastity girdle on one Mademoiselle Marie Layon. Was the lady his fiancée? A virgin relative under his guardianship? On the contrary, Ms. Layon was the mistress of this forewarned male. Paranoid Pierre, a frequent absentee landlord, covered the seams of Ms. Layon's chastity girdle with sealing wax, on which he then imposed his personal seal. Nutsy? Sure. But then she did have that inviting surname.

Paranoia can be carried to the grave. Suspicion that R.I.P. could be hogwash—and belief there's no rest for the wicked—lies with excavation of a cemetery in Austria during the nineteenth century. Unearthed was a female corpse locked in a chastity girdle. The key to her padlock has yet to surface.

This feudal device also brought cries of man's inhumanity to *man*, and, *perhaps*, woman. Who could put it more poetically than that great crusader against tyranny, bigotry, and cruelty—that bastion against injustice—the author Voltaire? Renowned for his satire, he also had his serious side. More on the frenzied side, Voltaire penned this irate poem to his mistress:

Le Cadenas—*The Padlock*

I Triumphed; Love was the master
And I was nearing these too brief instants

Of my happiness, and yours perhaps
But a tyrant wants to trouble our good time
He is your husband: a sexagenary prison keeper
He has locked the free sanctuary
Of your charms; and abusing our desires
Retains the key to the sojourn of pleasures . . .

Chastity belts still trap the entrance to vaginal estates in the twentieth century. They are rare—but so it goes with most handmade things. In England, as late as the 1970s, a forger (metal) still fashioned handmade chastity belts. On the fair end, he made chastity belts for both males and females. Those in need of this forger's address should seek another source. He's not in the *Blue Book;* we'll slip you that.

A fence to board up your vaginal property from an invader will be easier to locate. Ask around antique shops in Wales, New England, or Pennsylvania, for one of their eighteenth-century bundling boards. The Puritan's ethic was: Keep It Simple. In public life, simple functioned. In the privacy of sex, it was simpleminded, to say the least; to say the best, questionable.

To save on firewood, candles, dress-up clothes, and munchies for a cold night's courting, a gal was popped into bed with her intended with a bare board mounted between them. Honor-bound—there would be no leaps, from either side—records show illegitimacy soared in New England.

On the other side of the fence in frosty, puritan Wales, we get this report that, indeedy, there was no fence-hopping in Wales for the simple reason they were so lowly, it was beneath them:

> The lower order of people do actually carry on their love affairs in bed, and what would extremely astonish more polished lovers, they are carried on honorably, it being, at least, as usual . . . to go from the bed of

courtship to the bed of marriage as unpolluted and
maidenly as the Chloes of fashion; yet are not to con-
clude that this proceeds from their being less suscepti-
ble of the belle-passion than their betters; or the cold
air they breathe has froze the genial current of their
souls.

The above report comes from Mr. Pratt, an eighteenth-
century Welsh Puritan observer, obviously a simple soul,
who knew not from the complexities of making a flying leap
without freezing your balls.

If the bundling board was a yoke joke, not so the menace of the chastity sword placed between a man and a
woman to insure if any attack was made on her person, his
person would never survive intact to greet dawn's light.

Operating Expenses Within Reason

The Age of Reason brought the next board of directors
for management of quality control in vaginal estates—the
medical scientists. It was not easy. Christianity had its problems but, better believe it, it was well entrenched.

Their battle for a takeover got back up when modern
science made a big push to prove that Christianity's perspec-
tives on nature, with its corresponding controls on social
life, would not stand up under tests of experimental reason.
"Experimental" is our clue to medical science's *success* in
its takeover of vaginal plots—a reasonable assumption if we
examine the records.

Medical men backed the chastity belt to the hilt. Reason: It cut down on VD. And it cut off female masturbation,
from their reasoning a *very* unhealthy habit, a source for diseases going from A—Acne, B—Brain damage, and all between, down to the fatal Z—Zapped, totally. Unreasonably,
not every gal was into chastity belts. So, with good reason,
medical men came down to prescribing burn-out douches;

swabbing the vagina with serious chemicals; and/or castration of the vagina's delight, the clitoris.

And, lest we forget, their frigid weather reports were for the *healthy* vaginal zone. Mind you, if you look deep, all the above were a shot in the dark.

For centuries on end, the vagina was a depressed area, a controlled area, but decidedly depressed. What better reasoning could one ask than for medical science to place its major focus on inflationary rates in penile zones. Yes, there is good reasoning behind why, century after century, medical men didn't give their all for the vagina, other than a search for personal housing. Hey, the news can't be all bad.

ESCAPE CLAUSES, REAPPRAISAL, OPEN HOUSING,

RESURGENCE OF THE ENTREPRENEUR—

ALL IN ONE FUCKING CENTURY!

In the twentieth century, after two world wars that brought gals jobs and bucks, not to mention the right to vote and opportunities for a better education, in areas of the West women united to fight for sexual freedom. One heroic leader was Margaret Sanger, who battled for birth control. In 1950, Sanger's thirty-five-year battle for a woman's right to plan the size of her family challenged scientist Gregory Pincus to start his search for an oral contraceptive.

Shoving contraceptives up the vagina had been around long enough, since the sixteenth-century discovery of the condom, to prove you could take them or leave 'em. Most opted for a leave 'em. The vagina is sensitive, discriminating, excitable, fastidious, pliant, and downright touchy. If, instead, *she* could swig a pill, everything would be groovy.

The Pill has been around for a quarter of a century. And times for gals are indeed groovy. For a comparison report, look at Alfred Kinsey's finding in the late 1940s, ten years before the birth of the pill: By the age of sixteen, 40 percent of the males interviewed in the United States had lost their virginity, the figure for females was 3 percent. Now, a 1986 survey was taken in "the heart of screenland," Culver City, California, where 357 students between ages 11 to 13 said they were *sexually active;* between ages 14 to 18, 54 percent of 800 surveyed were sexually active. Average age for loss of virginity in the younger group broke down to 11.1 for boys; 11.7 for girls. In the older group, the average age for loss of virginity for boys was 13.2; for girls 14.6.

Groovy figures. Romantic ones? That's down the pike. Eleanor of Aquataine should be rocking in her grave; the Countess of Champagne belching "Bubbleheads."

Newfound freedom is rarely wise. It's a time to celebrate.

Has the celebration gone too far and too long? Look at it from this perspective. Individual management control of output from input made a gal boss of her precious vaginal estate for the first time since—well, let's say the Garden of Eden for the hell of it.

8

GETTING THE WORD OUT— WHERE IT WAS AT IN SEX ED

From antiquity down to the sixteenth century, it was believed by early biologists that the womb could move about in the body. If the womb moved from its proper place, it would lodge in a gal's throat, resulting in a chill of the heart, swooning, dizziness and suffocation. According to a medieval sex ed book, the cause of the womb separating from the vagina was a profusion of spoiled, poisonous menstrual blood. To avoid womb suffocation, women, young or old, were advised to have frequent sexual intercourse. Since young women were filled with moisture, the more sex the better.

De Secretis Mulierum by Albert Magnus tells us

this string to a healthy womb creates a Catch-22 operation:

> . . . Young women, when they are full of such matter,
> feel a strong desire for sex just because this matter
> abounds in them. It is therefore a sin, in nature, to keep
> them from it and stop them from having sex with the
> man they favor, although [their doing so] is a sin ac-
> cording to accepted morality. But this is another ques-
> tion.

The gals swallowed it—those *fortunate* enough to get
wind of a cure for wandering wombs—but morality didn't.
Sex ed was a battle then, especially for the young, and it
remains a battle, a very sick battle, as of this writing.

As a science, sex education for the young is less than a
half-century old. So how did kids down through the centuries learn where it was at? It's a huge question and a big
world. Let's draw a bead on one era and a minuscule area—
English nursery rooms and playgrounds of the eighteenth
and nineteenth centuries.

In the nursery, through playful chants and songs, tots
were taught functions of the body. And brainwashed with
morals, morals, morals. Let's start at the beginning—Adam
and Eve:

> *Adam and Eve and Pinch-me-tight*
> *Went down to the river to bathe.*
> *Adam and Eve were drowned,*
> *Who do you think was saved?*

To make sure they got the picture there were hand-fin-
ger signals, starting with:

> *Here is the church, here is the steeple;*
> *Open the door, here are the people.*

Here is the parson going upstairs,
Here he is saying his prayers.

Graduating to:

Here are the lady's knives and forks,
Here is the lady's table,
Here is the lady's looking-glass,
And here is the baby's cradle

As tots moved out from the nursery into the playgrounds—streets and alleys—older kids took up their sex ed with bawdy chants, often under a guise of rhythmic songs sung during communal games.

For the new kid on the street the chant was innocence itself, a step up on the nursery tune "Jack and Jill":

There was a little boy and a little girl,
Lived in an alley,
Says the little boy to the little girl,
Shall I, or shall I?

Says the little girl to the little boy,
What shall we do?
Says the little boy to the little girl,
I will kiss you!

Sometimes the chant was a warning:

The little girl in the lane, that couldn't speak plain,
Cried "Gobble, gobble gobble."
The man on the hill, that couldn't stand still,
Went hobble, hobble, hobble.

Sometimes "Face the music, kid":

> As I was going up the hill,
> I met with Jack the Piper;
> And all the tune that he could play
> Was, "Tie up your petticoats tighter."

> I tied them once, I tied them twice,
> I tied them three times over:
> And all the song that he could sing
> Was, "Carry me safe to Dover."

Sometimes practical:

> Some to make hay, diddle, diddle,
> Some to thresh corn,
> Whilst you and I, diddle, diddle,
> Keep ourselves warm.

Some pissed off:

> Young Roger came a tapping at Dolly's window,
> Thumpetty, thumpetty, thump!
> He asked to come in, she bawled out her "No!"
> Frumpetty, frumpetty, frump!

Some wishful thinking:

> As I was going o'er London Bridge,
> And peeped through a nick,
> I saw four and twenty ladies,
> Riding on a stick.

Some a look down life's road:

> *Shall I go with thee pretty fair maid?*
> *Do if you will, sweet Sir.*
> *What if I lay you down on the ground?*
> *I will rise up again, sweet sir.*
> *What if I do bring you with child?*
> *I will bear it, sweet Sir.*
> *And who will you have for father for your child?*
> *You shall be his father, sweet Sir.*
> *What will you do for whittles for your child?*
> *His father will be a tailor, sweet Sir.*

Some a blind gal's bluff:

> *There was a little maid and she was afraid*
> *That her sweetheart would come on to her;*
> *So she went to bed, covered up her head,*
> *And fastened her door with a skewer!*

Some a juicy revenge:

I have been to market, my lady, my lady;
Then you have not been to the fair, says pussy, says pussy,
I have bought me a rabbit, my lady, my lady,
Then you did not buy a hare, says pussy, says pussy,
I roasted it, my lady, my lady,
Then you did not boil it, says pussy, says pussy,
I eat it, my lady, my lady,
And I'll eat you, says pussy, says pussy.

Some laid out a mess:

> *Little pretty Nancy girl,*
> *She sat upon a green,*

Scouring of her candlesticks,
They were not very clean.
Her cupboard that was musty,
Her table that was dusty;
And pretty little Nancy girl,
She was not very lusty.

Some a career-move success:

Elsie Marley is grown so fine,
She won't get up to serve her swine,
But lies in bed till eight or nine,
And surely does take her time . . .

Elsie Marley wore a straw hat,
But now she's got a velvet cap,
She may thank the Lambton boys for that.
Do you know Elsie Marley, honey? . . .

The sailors they do call for flip,
As soon as they come from the ship,
And then begin to dance and skip
To the tune of "Elsie Marley," honey.

Some therapeutic:

Margery Mutton-Pie and Johnny Bo-peep,
They met together in Gracechurch Street,
In and out, in and out, over the way,
"Oops," said Johnny, it's chop-nose day.

Some downright tragic:

He loves me,
He don't,

> He'll have me,
> He won't,
> He would if he could,
> But he can't
> So he don't.

Some resigned:

> I had a little husband,
> No bigger than my thumb;
> I put him in a pint-pot
> And there I bade him drum . . .

Your alley education was complete when you sunk to:

> When I was a young Maid, and
> wash't my Mother's dishes,
> I put my finger in my hole and
> pluck't out little Fishes.

After alley graduation you knew where it was at.

What about deprived tots and kids? The upper-class lassies and laddies? In nurseries, they were listening to their old-maid nannies croaking "Three Little Kittens Lost Their Mittens" and were bounced to "Little Bo-Peep Lost Her Sheep." Never a hint of lost virginity. With good reason—nannies did not have vaginas. So—what you don't have, you can't lose, and the less said the better.

Outgrowing the nursery, upper-class lassies were tutored at home by virgin governesses, who, knowing not from it, spoke not of it at all. Not so for upper-class laddies. They where in public schools being pumped with chivalrous tales—Victorian edition. In their prep schools, they were being prepared to fight the Dragon Sex.

The Return to Camelot, Chivalry and the English Gen-

tleman gives us the noble routine handed down through noble tales to little noble gents. Tennyson's version of chivalry, "Live pure, speak true, right wrong, follow the King" was "the established ethic of chivalry, . . . and approved of by the public schools and, not surprisingly, by the Queen." Speak true did not include speak blue, for this book tells us, "Lancelot and Guenevere clearly presented problems. . . . Adultery is never even hinted at; in the final drama Lancelot and Guenevere are accused of a mysterious 'treason,' the nature of which is never explained."

In the mystical land of Victorian chivalry, the vagina was a mystery—apparently, there were areas where it didn't exist. It disappeared in noble lassies, and if noble ladies possessed one, it was pure as driven snow; that is, frigid.

In their fantasy world, to promote nonsex ed, the public schools got back up from the troops. First came Baden-Powell's newly formed army, the Boy Scouts, where the mere thought of sex was annihilated in icy tubs and showers. Later came the troops of older lads eighteen and up (fifteen to eighteen could be associate members) marching to the drumming of the Alliance of Honor, honor-bound "to impress men and youths the necessity of living pure lives."

The Return to Camelot describes the dragons fought by Young Knights of the Alliance:

> Masturbation and fornication were the two dragons . . . to fight. Doctors told them how sexual abstinence was compatible with perfect health. Explorers wrote about Scott of the Antarctic and how "we may safely assert that among the heroes of that dreadful journey . . . there were no victims of the vice which the Alliance seeks to combat." The Bishop of Durham distinguished between "admirers of women" who were "frankly animal" and "reverencers of woman who look upon her as God's masterpiece of truth and virtue, made to be man's guiding star, his better self . . ." [etc, etc, yawn]. Members were told to think of "the sacredness of your sister's

body" and to remember that every woman, however low she has fallen, was likely to be someone's sister.

You will get no record here of what the alley songs said about someone's/anyone's sister.

The Alliance branched out to sixty-seven countries. It died after World War II, except for a branch in South Africa, which needs all the help it can get.

It didn't take a world war to topple Victorian nonsex ed. It took one man's throwback revolt: Sigmund Freud's theory that sexual instinct, sexual drive, and sexual act do not start with the approach of puberty—they start in the cradle. For cannon fodder, Freud trotted out the little buggers—maintaining these early instincts, drives, and acts were not only normal, they were a healthy goal to achieve hedonistic *pleasure*, and if this goal was thwarted, a little bugger was doomed to a life of fixation. (That is, a rigid insistence for a regular bowel movement could fixate one for life at the anal level of satisfaction. This anal complex—that feces were to be tidy bundles, timely and properly ejected and not squished at random all over the joint—could fixate the personality in a variety of nasty satisfactions and goals, such as stashing your bucks and keeping the house neat.)

The fix was on. Parents, guilt-ridden, turned to science for solutions. But science knew from not. Till Freud dropped his feces bomb, no one in science stooped to examine what those little buggers were into down there. Queried and curious, science poked around in the cradle and the nursery. Surfacing, the scientific stoolies sung a shocking tale.

In the cradle, science discovered infants had plucky orgasms and spunky erections. Graduated to the nursery, tots wanted straightforward answers—which they never got—to: Why do you call Billy's a "stick" and mine a "hole?" How do *you* make babies? Why must I call Billy's a "thing" and mine a "nothing?"

Did revelations of sexual activity in the cradle followed by gamy questions on "How Come?" bring an uproar—from either science or parent—to get sex ed on the road before those little buggers got it all wrong and ruined what little they had goin for 'em? Forget it. Better to turn out fixated adults than to chance opening that can of twisty worms.

But the worm will turn, and so does the pelvis. And, so too does the record on the machine.

In the United States, in the mid 1940s, mobs of teenage girls changed the scene for sex ed. They migrated, like hypnotized lemmings, into what are now the playgrounds of the twentieth century—concert pavilions and halls. It was a natural progression, looking back. Teenage sex ed, in a few generations, had moved off the streets and tuned in to signals sent over radios, films, and record players. At first, the signals were adult and subtle, like that teaser "What Is This Thing Called Love," zeroing in on "Night and Day, You Are the One." Then down came signals outright erotic. Picture if you will: On one side of the record you do your solo tuned in to "Temptation"; on the flip side, your fantasy duet to "Begin the Beguine."

Ahhhh! Finally, down the pike, came reality. "The Pelvis" gyrated on the scene. Elvis' beat was lewd and naughty, his delivery blue and erotic, his attire decidedly ballsy, his lips definitely pursed for your endless kiss, for certain his steamy eyes bedrolled you. But, in the end, it was Presley's pelvis that grabbed you.

Elvis was *too* much! Parents shivered in disgust. Educators wanted to throw the book at him. Churchmen did. As for those kids, they were busy rockin' and rollin'—who now was tuned into listenin'?

Most teenage gals in the fifties knew where their vaginas were at; many used it; few, however, knew *how* to use it. Elvis rolled it out there for all the gals to see. And the world was never the same again.

Rock and Roll was a volcanic action/reaction that erupted over most of this globe in the sixties, seventies, and continues its slide into some unlikely areas; that is, China in the eighties. No one can spot the world as it spins. Nowadays, one has to be blind not to spot the spin of the pelvis.

For sex ed, no one beat the beat of Elvis.

Where is sex ed at today in the West? Who needs it? Kids now know the action.

How about reaction? Despite the availability of The Pill—and the bypass of ye ole flexible standby—the condom—teenage pregnancies and abortions are soaring. The beauty, and the pain, of youth is, they for one are, invincible. Kids today echo back, "That's the chance you take."

It has been ever thus. What has not been ever thus is the plague of fatal AIDS. In 1985, when *The Male Member* was published, the number of those infected with AIDS in the United States was approaching 7,000. In 1987, when *The Female Member* goes to press, that figure will read well over 40,000. In the 7,000 victims recorded earlier, the transference of AIDS through heterosexual activity was 1 percent. Of those 40,000-plus victims now, heterosexually transference, as a base figure, will approach 4 percent. Estimates from experts vary; whichever you choose to believe, they are no less alarming. In 1986, estimates of heterosexual transmission varied from 1200 to 2300. Estimated figures by 1991, for heterosexually transmitted AIDS, vary from 15,000 to 23,000. And deaths are estimated to go as high as 179,000 for all victims of AIDS.

In late 1986, the United States Surgeon General advised sex ed start in the schools for pupils nine years and up (lessons on the disease as early as third grade), with the focus on AIDS protection; that is, celibacy, monogamy, and condoms. In 1987, the Surgeon General has a war on his hands in lower schools.

Near 80 percent of the high schools around the country

have instituted *some* form of sex ed; that is, info on pregnancy, contraception, sexual relationships, and sexually transmitted diseases. In the latter, many focus now on protection from exposure to AIDS via celibacy or use of the condom.

Take as a possible given, sex ed now in all schools: What about the dropouts? What about smart asses who won't sit tight for a lecture? What about the gambler—AIDS is for the next guy? What about those who get a thrill playing sexual Russian roulette? And last, far from least, the kids in private schools where sex ed is banned, especially the condom?

Take as fact: In two counties bordering on Washington, D.C., where sex ed classes are available, after parental written permission, only 8 percent of the high school students sign up each year. A school spokesman, quoted in the *Washington Post* in March 1987, says, "Given all the push for awareness, the current state of affairs is kids, by choice, don't take these courses." Why? Across the board comes back: I'm too busy; Not interested; I don't need that course to get into college; and, I don't need it. In the District of Columbia, sex ed is a one-year required course for graduation, but the D.C. dropout rate is in a persistent dive.

The obvious solution to get the word out on AIDS and preventive measures to kids of all ages and interests is the television ad. Unfortunately, on television condoms are a can of worms.

In most nations, the condom, until the plague of AIDS, was unmentionable in all forms of "respectable" media. In the United States, you heard "fuck" on pay television films years before you heard "condom," "anal sex," or the "passive/receiver" on talk shows.

In 1987 in Britain, Sweden, and France, ads for condoms have expanded to television. They're viewed as lifesaving business, with ads showing women buying condoms and laying it on the line before they engage in sex. A skyrocket increase in sales of condoms to European women proves the word is out—gals are buying the message: "It's your self-protection."

At the same time in the fast-lane United States, condom ads are a no-no. In 1987, top television networks hedged, saying many of their viewers would find condom ads a turn-off. Their view nationwide—in local slots—that's your busting headache. Prediction is the networks will turn around. But, how many people, especially among the young, contract AIDS as network honchos stew about propriety, yet saturate viewers with the glories of violence and trash sex?

Radio is, for now, an easier barrier to break the taboo on condom ads. But, a speedier method might be that old standby, song.

Time has proven, kids dig getting sex ed through song. Their songs. So, we'll need cool, cool words. And one damn cool singer. If this pendulum swings, Elvis rock in your grave.

9

PACKAGING SEX: CIRCA 1200—1960

"Coition is a slight attack of apoplexy."

*—Democritus of Abdera
(460–370 B.C.)*

Some image. Yet, as a consultant for what lies ahead, Democritus was on top of it. *The Encyclopaedia Britannica* describes this Greek philosopher as anticipating ". . . theories of the indestructibility of matter and of the conservation of matter. . . . Atoms and Void are for Democritus the two ultimate realities." But if we examine his vision of coition, we see Democritus also had a picture of the image that would be coming down in the packaging of sex from the fourth century to the sexual revolution of the 1960s.

The taboo of sex, targeted for centuries as "the bedrock of evil" or downwrong "unhealthy," was fought by the lower classes through language. Uneducated, they resorted to "dirty words." As image consultants for sex—combating the heavyweights, church and science—their low-class dirt campaign poured into every crevice of sexual experience.

And gals, as the foundation for coitus, were the first target in a dirty-language marketing strategy. If we look at their oppositions' "evil, unhealthy" image for sex, dirty jargon, by blowing this image to the height of *nasty filth*, balances out: Ridicule can be "good, clean, fun." So, for a few pages, ignore the scrub of a sexual revolution and wallow in a dirt campaign to sell gals as sex objects.

To cover the stretch of this dirty road we have greased the mechanics for a breakdown.

Seat Covers
Nestle-cock
Tickle tail
Loose
Warm bit

Classy Chassis
Amoret
Quean quiff
Bummerkeh
Franion
Amorosa
Scate.

Generators
High flyer
Willing tit
A cinch

Intake Valve
Hot tongue
Soft roll
Hot stuff
Gooseberry pudding
Bit of jam
A peach
Hot tomato
Hot tamale
Pie

Let Her Rip
Easy virtue
Dangerous Curves
Quick on the draw
Walk-up fuck

Automatic Choke
Ball buster

Automatic Choke (cont.)
Gash
Free for all
Cleaver
Bomb shell

Resonator
Cleopatra bites snake
Sheba

Yank the Engine
Baloney
Piece of ass
Easy meat
Pigmeat
Town punch
Mutton
Blimp
Pig

Floor Mats
Good girl
Pleaser
Easy
Dry lay
Cuddle bunny

Wiper Blade Refills
Flapper
Loose woman
Table grade
Uptight
Piece of stray
Groupie

Wiper Blade Refills (cont.)
Bimbo
Hairy bit

Distributor Caps
Hussy
Fornicatress
Floosey
Chippy
Hobby horse
Wench
Deb generate
Substation

Pick Up & Go
Cleave
Trot hot
Bobtailed
Nysot

Crankshafts
Yes girl
B-girl
Libertine
Strollop

Brake & Run
Gobble prick
Goober grabber
Rutter
Piece of tail

Spark Plugs
Hump
Ho! Ho! Ho!

Spark Plugs (cont.)
Glutz
A spread
Big twenty

Rear-Ended
Open-arse
Bangster
A bundle

Butterfly Nuts
Wag your tail
Light of love
Hobby

Catalytic Converters
Adulteress
Charity dame
Brood
Suburb sinner

Wheel Spokes
Low rent
Charity stuff
A Sex-job
Gay

Shocks
Hogminny
Split tail

Go Lights
Gay in the groin
Gig
Gigletting

Go Lights (cont.)
Gill flurt
Good lay
Graduate
Gixie

Voltage Meters
A poll
A hummer
Push over

Engine Blocks
Goes whole hog
Frying pan
Letching piece

Dead Battery
Madamoi-zook
Calico queen
Miss Horner

Joy Sticks
Tom's rig
Smock toy
Plaything
Giglot
Giggler

Exterior Trim
Loose kirtle
Dress goods
Light skirts
Round heels
Hat rack
Short heels

Exterior Trim (cont.)
Piece of snatch
Shagtress

Credit Card Welcome
Fad cattle
Hot number
Horns to sell

Pickup Truck
Easy rider
Tramp
Slotted job
Tube

Experimental Model
Puta
Adultera
Tit
Sleez
Nit

Complete Overhaul
Soft jaw
Biffer
Push over
Dirty leg
Poke
Biter
Gay in the groin

Import Parts
Scupper
Light frigate
Rig mutton

Import Parts (cont.)
Flap
Athanasian wench

Flat Tire
Slack
Soft lay
Bike
Hike
Flat out

Cruise Control
Snatch
Clap trap
Coming wench
Fly
Trot

Check Oil Filter
Instant jelly
Fizzgig
Bunny cake
Quail
Sex pot
Stuff

Nuts & Bolts
Band bangster
Jazz baby
Belly lass

Semiautomatic
Sleeping partner
Easy lay
Easy mark

132

Heavy Duty
Knock
Light housewife
Grass back
Grind
Dead & easy

Differentials
Charity girl
Trash
Bed bug
Beetle
Lady bird
Alley cat
Taint
Ass

Differentials (cont.)
Bed bunny
Hot pants
Flirtigigs
Hook alley
Play girl

Peak Performance
Hunk
Hot member
Shtup
Tickles Toby
Dead easy
Hot lay
Warming pan
Pickup

For gals feelin' horny the dirt really flew.

Double-Clutching
Horn happy
Bulling
Tickle
Ranting
Turned on

Brake Shoes
Ramstudious
Be on blob
Itchy pants
Wet
Mannish
Proud

Japanese Imports?
Maris Appentes

Japanese Imports? (cont.)
Affy
Liquorous
Accensus libidine
Whisk telt
Amative
Concupiscent

Give Her the Gas
In the mood
Rammy
Fuckish
Cock happy
Ruttish

Cranked
Pruny

Cranked (cont.)
Randy
Fuckin' mad
Oncoming

Voltage Regulator
Full of gism
Bone on
Hunky
Prime
Purse proud

Tailgate Party
Salt
Juicy
Hot in the biscuit
Be mustard
Tumbling ripe
Peas in the pot
In season
Mashed
On for one's greens

Overheated
Hot-assed
Hot-blooded

Overheated (cont.)
Fire not put out
Gamy

Needs Lubrication
Feel fuzzy
Rusty
Feel hairy
Het up
Lickerish

White Walls
Constitutionally inclined to
gallantry

Last-Year's Model
Sexed up
Be blotty
Hot and bothered
Chucked
Have an itch in the belly
Touchy

Combustion Chamber
Hunk of tail
Hunk of skirt
Hunk of ass
Hunk of butt

But gals were not alone on the dirt road rerouting of sex. There were these dirty old men out there just waiting to letch on to them.

Chop Shops
Womanizers
Thrumpsters

Chop Shops (cont.)
Whisker splitters
Pelters

134

Chop Shops (cont.)
Rump splitters
Pinch buttocks
Meat hounds
Knockers
Flesh mongers

Front-Ended
Jumbler
Dolly Mopper
Swiver
Wet noodle
Old wet goose

Automatic Starters
Casanovas
Bluebeards
Don Juans
Lotharios

Crankcase
Whoremaster
Whore hopper
Whore hound
Whore monger

Clunkers
Adulterers
Leachers
Sons of Venus
Town stallions
Rattlers
Swingers
Squires of the body
Rakes

Howlers
Fox hunters
Cock fighters
Alley cats
Fishmongers
Tomcats
Hootchees

Run It into the Ground
Riders
Rangers
Mouse hunters
Shifter
Holers
Girl trappers
Bum fiddlers

Blew a Gasket
Finger man
Twat faker
Tummy tickler
Tug mutton
Smells smock
Loose in the hilt
Finger fucker
Dribbles & drooles
Poopster
Pinch bottom
Quim stickler

Lemons
Performers
Leg lifters
Sharp shooters
Punkers

Lemons (cont.)
Gay men
D.O.M.s

Overheated
Hot nuts
Hot pants
Rattle cap

Chokers
High priest of papos
Eater of forbidden fruit

Tow Trucking
Wencher
Gap stopper
Basher
Ballocker
Fleece monger
Town rake

Exhaust System
Bed pressers
Lusty guts
Parish bull
Sexual athlete
Woman chaser
Town bull
Headhunter
Stallion
Stud

Power Antennas
Philanderer
Tough Cat

Power Antennas (cont.)
Rooster
Faggoteer

Mechanic
Make out artist
Tweak
Peach orchard bore
Animal
Grouser
Feather bed soldier
Faggotmonger
Gully raker
Fuckster
Rumper
King of clubs
Stringer
Diver
Rutter
Scortator
Mr. Horner
Cocksmith
Game cock

Racers
Chippy chaser
Eager beaver
Cocksman

Bumper Guards
Belly bumpers
Bustmaker
Ass man
Skirt foist

Steering Hose
Quail Hunter
Gin shepherd
Dundering rake
Fleece hunter

Body Shop
Gusseteer
Skin dog
Gash hound
Kid stretcher
Smockster
Ladies' tailor
Button Man
Leather dresser
Figure maker

Interior Trim
Sporty
Flower fancie
Shag
Bird's nester
Hair monger
Rounder
Pinch cunt
Mutton cove

Tire Mounts
Amorist
Buck up
Horseman

But, despite the sexual revolution, there remains to this day a hoary-headed joke tagged the condom. A mini history of the condom was reviewed in *The Male Member*. The long and the short of it: The condom has never been easy to sell and still harder to promote. It's so unpopular, the inventor of the condom has yet to surface and every nation denies it a birth record. In this shuffle, the condom has been passed around as: the English envelope; the French letter; the Spanish letter; the American letter; the enemy of your choice letter, et cetera. Note: nary a drop of the term condom.

Today, and for uncountable tomorrows, in a battle against AIDS, the condom is the only sex tool we have to fight this fatal plague. Yet, it is near to impossible to promote the condom. The media shudders at a mere whisper of advertising *the taboo*. Today television ads for douches get on prime time—only because the term douche is never dropped and the pitch is disguised to sell: "freshness"; "a dainty deodorant"; "a hygienic pick-me-up," under masquerade of a sly, knowing wink exchanged between savvy mom and her very with-it daughter. As for ads for "sanitary napkins," you could use the same sales jargon to sell maxi-strength Band-Aids.

When it comes down to beating the taboo of condom ads on television, we should take a lesson from the repackaged image of the douche and "sanitary napkins." True, some local television stations are sliding in condoms under Public Service Announcements. When was the last time you listened to a P.S.A. *and* took action? Network television advertising is the only way to go if you want *fast* nationwide sales today. Learning lessons, for AIDS, come late, if at all. The solution: Don't fight the networks, join 'em.

Bury, forever the monicker Condom and antique nicknames such as One-piece Overcoat, Shower Cap, Eel Skin, Latex, Phallic Symbol, Lubie, Diving Suit, Balloon, Port Said Garter, Scum Bag, Cheater, Phallic Thimble, and, for all that's sacred, scrap Rubber.

For males, trade up to a something that signals high performance, goes the course, and produces value for your dollar. For a shot, let's bounce around the ring of "Zerk Fitting"—a rip-off from auto mechanics, meaning the place where the grease gun is inserted to a ball joint during a lube job.

Image makers might also check out the jargon the auto supply industry uses to push thousands of items geared for performance and reliability. With a little imagination, and *under a new name,* there is world of material there to hitch on to for an unbeatable sales pitch that the media could find little to fault for all family-oriented advertising.

Try these on for a gross purchase:

Computerized alignment for thrust angle
See your way clear

138

Wiper refills up to 18-inch sizes
30,000-mile wear warranty (for gross purchases)
Protectant that beautifies
Plush, simulated sheepskin covers
For low-bucket seating
All-season filters
Low-cost refills
You install what we sell
Improves steering and handling
Saves on wear and tear
Rides like a stretch limo
Pressure-gauged to manufacturer's specs
Recommended for standard ignitions
That tangle-free booster cable
Engine dress-up kit
Medium, large, and extra large (small size special order)
Valve Saver
It's a spare tire in a can
Inflates and seals
Spray-and-choke cleaner
Clam-o-matic
Degreaser plus spot remover
Brake fluid and sealant
Power-steering fluid
Double-stitched driving gloves
Swivel grip to clear exhaust
Heavy-duty supports won't sag
Shockproof
Handles twice the load of ordinary coil springs
Strut cartridges
Bias-belted
Holds up to five quarts
Set timing and adjust speed (where applicable)
Rust and corrosion resistant
Top or side terminal—your choice

Ignition cap and rotor kit
Master cylinder with rebuildable part in trade
Mounts on turn signal
Fast forward and eject
Pick-up pockets to carry your gear
Super strength for racing boost
For pickup truck pass through sliding
Will not rust, chip, or dent
Shatterproof guaranteed
Flow-thru thread design for all-weather performance
"A"-rated traction
Maximum protection against viscosity and thermal break-
   down
Lined with genuine grizzly lining (honest Injun)
Carry-out sale price $5.95—installed $95.95

   The mechanics pitch too male-oriented? A "Zerk Fitting" will never grab gals, and that mechanic jargon far
from romantic? To sell gals, *tell them* that the "layered look"
is *in, in, in!*
   Do your pitch with fashion yuck that sucks—the gals in:

Comes only in cherry red
Pullover knots smartly to the side
Machine-washable, gentle cycle
Front and rear darts
Imported stretch belts
Casual pullover touched with collar ruffle
For added flair, the go-anywhere classic design
Stylish satin slide—dry clean only
A Peter Pan collar with detachable bow
Herringbone weave, the timeless basic
Sheering on sleeve and collar for a finished look
One size fits all

Comes in honey beige, nude, and blush pink
The all-around 3/4 length
Fully cushioned insole for all-day comfort
A winner—the tulip-hemmed tunic
Pocket blazers that go anywhere
In hard-to-find sizes
Please check sizes and colors carefully
Stylish separates—chic, sleek, the way to go
Exceptionally tailored raincoats—when it pours you're covered
Jacket elegance with contrasting piping
Windowpane checks for a look of staying power
Feather-light uppers—add a touch of texture to your day
Expandable wrap style
Pullover sweater with elasticized waist and cuffs
The nautical look for your cruise
For the price of one, a knit threesome
A dry-clean coat with detachable lining
Ribbed eye-catching crepe for a fit without a wrinkle
Skimp-style sweater with inseam pocket
Flattering float for the unique woman
Oriental-inspired frog closures
Dramatic jumpsuit
High-necked Victorian style—timeless solution for all-around dressing
The demi-boot for slip-on ease
Rises to a 2-inch heel for walking ease
Proportioned pants in colors to go
You'll applaud the comfort
Casual clam digger
Hand-loomed chic shell
Heartwarming style—heart-shaped cuffs
The boned corselet with front and back support
The breezy delight of a skirted swimsuit
Body briefer with a hooked crotch

The soft separate that packs like a dream
That interchangeable accent you can't be without

As for unisex television imagery: Package condoms under "Closet Wonders." Then slide into:

Trendy triangle shapes that should grab you
Storage for springtime turtlenecks
How to pack double-knit jump suits
Popcorn-stitch for that special look
Psuedo-snakeskin in natural only
The houndstooth jacket you've been searching for
The web belt that hides a multiple of sins
Fits better without flattening, distorting or squeezing
Helps to ease crushing and wrinkling
Perfect choice for shopping, entertaining, and at-home relax-
    ing
You don't have to be a magician to double your space
Hook on to any existing rod, holds up to 40 pounds
Gift wrap available
Allows me to see all my jackets at a glance
Perfect for college dorms and mobile life-styles
Flexible hangers—they carry more than you could dream
Lets you lay back and enjoy and still get three-speed action
Nonsticky, can be used daily on all skin types
Splash, no more ends mop-up
Professional look without the usual mess
Do *not* peel back the protective film
No scissors necessary!
Skimp and Scamps fit you like a second skin
Side panels for that extra stretch
The bag that lets you get your essentials quickly, with ease
The tubular design makes it a cinch to slide on, no straps, or
    buckles to adjust or protrude, so it isn't noticeable un-
    der his clothing

Designed to grip everything, an anchor for every depth
The perfect suction cup!!
Satisfaction guaranteed or your money back!

A word of warning when you're producing your television scripts. Before your network wraps it up: Don't forget to drop that sly knowing wink, or no one will guess what the fuck it is you're really selling—which will make your boss *very* happy; and, a lot of us out there, *very, very* sick.

But the subtle approach for condom ads is not what a majority of American television viewers want or need. Not if we take as a basis a poll taken by the *Washington Post* and ABC news in March 1987. Out of 1,511 questioned, "Three-quarters of those surveyed said they favored television advertising of condoms to prevent the spread of AIDS."

That the hammer of persistent publicity is needed—to put the condom in action as opposed to buying condoms and putting them on the shelf for some future rainy day when your rubbers will *really* come in handy—is evident in the following scary statistics. In that same poll, 96 percent believed intimate sexual contact (along with sharing intravenous needles and blood transfusions) was how one contacted AIDS from someone who had it; but only half of the respondents, who were single and who were 35 and under, had changed their sexual habits to protect themselves (condoms or monogamy); and 73 percent said they were not afraid that they would become infected.

In that same week in March 1987, the *Washington Post* interviewed a street prostitute after a chilling statistic that 50 percent of the female prostitutes in the District of Columbia were infected with the AIDS virus. The street pro, who says it's condom or no go, claimed half her dates are married dudes and the majority of those try to talk her out of use of the condom. And then she wonders if these dudes

143

want to play Russian roulette, why do they make their wives play, unknowingly, the same perilous game.

Now the choke news. In February 1987, the *Journal of the American Medical Society* released a report based on a study carried out at the University of Miami School of Medicine, monitoring the health and sex habits of forty-five adults with AIDS and their spouses. The study's principal author says, ". . . the use of the condom decreases the risk of transmission, but it's not 100%." Out of ten couples in which one spouse had AIDS and used condoms regularly, three of the uninfected spouses developed AIDS and, overall, sexual transmission of AIDS was high, with more than half of the spouses showing evidence of infection. And *oral sex, for women, increased their risk.*

One of the major problems with condoms, according to Fischl, is that "People don't know how to use them."

Some rules: Condoms deteriorate after several months; some brands are better, stronger, than others; the condom should be in place before intercourse; and during intercourse if a condom breaks or comes off, the woman should *immediately* douche and for added protection use a spermicide.

And, to play it real safe, drop oral sex.

It's a whole new ball game, but these rules have a sad, but oh so familiar ring. The tragic toll: ". . . any man's death diminishes me, because I am involved in mankind: and therefore never send to know for whom the bell tolls; it tolls for thee."

10

MYSTERIOUS BOOKKEEPING FOR VAGINAL ACTIVITY IN HISTORY

Do vaginal accounts show a return on their historical investments? Is a miss as good as a milestone?

For those holding prominent portfolios (i.e., vaginal powerhouses, Salome, Cleopatra, Catherine the Great), you read stock reports that skyrocket off their sheets. How accurate are these reports? Who knows after centuries of diddling with accounts now listed as public holdings. If books don't jive, balance it this way: At least some attempt was made to come up with a vaginal historical audit.

But, what happens to the accounts on private holdings—vaginas, pumping with all their steam, plus a loving heart, for males who shaped history? Pal, in these areas of strategic vaginal activity, we're looking at historical bankruptcy.

Bankruptcy, that is, if there are any accounts—much less books—kept at all.

In an effort to balance these strategic vaginal accounts let us move for an audit. And, since core memory is down on private vaginal holdings, we're looking at a labor of love.

What zapped core memory? One: pirating of vaginal accounts by stockholders who, to a man, prefer keeping their deposits secret. Two: a glitch due to a massive overload brought on by feminists claiming vaginal accounting, back to recorded times, has been coded under "Fringe Benefits" or, worse, "Perks." Horizontal integration, over this broad expanse of time, has sparked a malfunction signal in all vaginal software printouts. Wiping this glitch could well take a century, since repairmen sit on their behinds whining: "Double damn, it's the feminist bookkeeping that's full of holes."

To bypass handicap of pirating and the glitch, let us vote for a personal audit on a few strategic vaginal accounts; then via a summary analysis, determine whether, indeed, these private vaginal holdings are getting a screwed credit report and remain historical ghosts to this day.

Ghost of Vagina #1:
The Vaginal Account of Louise Colet

Are balance sheets juggled by bookkeepers to wipe the deposits made by Louise Colet, Gustave Flaubert's mistress, for inspiration in the development of his character Emma Bovary? Are accountants for *Madame Bovary* over the years crediting Flaubert as sole depositor in the creation of a heroine that has flamed for a century as a beacon in modern literature?

One of the enigmas in the history of modern literature is

why, after publication of his Realist breakthrough novel, did Flaubert, in answer to a question on the source for his haunting heroine—and central character—claim, "Madame Bovary is me."

Biographers and literary historians come up with a host of noble excuses for Flaubert's pussy simple response. The slice of a few: artistic license; evasion of nosy parkers; regret for his use of a "fallen woman's" tragic tale of adultery and suicide; his noble attempt to protect another "fallen woman" currently under exile from society for her blatant acts of adultery; that, in "soul," he was Emma Bovary; and an assortment of other spooky entries.

These noblesse oblige recorders go on, at great length, documenting Flaubert's haunting heroine as the work of genius and a poetic creation. They ignore their blaring imbalance as they proceed to document, and acclaim, that Flaubert wrote only after scrupulous research, personal observation, or experience to record, without invention, the human condition and human reactions to conditions—in his slavish effort to eradicate the fantasy of the romantic style from every possible crevice of his Realist novel.

Their subtotal reads: Everything in Madame Bovary was either experienced by Flaubert or was sought out by him before ever putting pen to paper. But, nowhere in their data do we get corrected the imbalance of how it came to be that Flaubert, a full-blooded male *and* an avowed unromantic, came up with his X-ray portrait for the ultimate romantic, the erotic, dependent Emma Bovary. In their spooky bookkeeping, we are expected to believe a total that balances out: Emma's day-by-day existence of living life on the romantic edge descended, like a gift from above, into Flaubert's mind and flowed with the light of truth on page after page of his manuscript—a manuscript dedicated to be the first novel written from life and backed by the realism of research and experience.

When next you hear a scholar weep, "Bodice-rippers, those fantasies, reap more than mine," console, after a wink punctuated by a cultured sigh, with, "That's the price you pay, locked in your ivory tower amid the clouds of scholarly bookkeeping."

So, where did Flaubert do his research—to suck in the reality of a woman obsessed with romantic passion and the pain of repeated rejection? In the vaginal well, and the tears and useless pleading of his only mistress, in fact the only woman in his life other than casual sex partners, Louise Colet.

And how do we prove it? Letters. Letters. Letters. Not, grievous to report, Louise Colet's letters to Flaubert. All—hundreds—were destroyed by Flaubert's niece after his death because they contained "too many horrors." Instead, and best possibly to prove our point, Flaubert's loving, and not so loving, responses to Colet as he recorded his, near daily, progress on the writing of *Madame Bovary*.

These letters, in the three-figure mark, date back to well before Flaubert ever dreamed of writing *Madame Bovary*. But it's Flaubert's responses to Colet, during the writing of his book, that document his touchstone to create, from real life, his complex—but oh so real—heroine. His letters record the evolution of his portrait of Emma Bovary in her desperate, devious search for love and a richer life while, almost daily, he reads correspondence from his mistress relating her daily existence under mounting debts and pleas for a return of passion from him.

In this audit summary on the Louise Colet account are itemized Flaubert's IOU's never repaid to Colet and, mysteriously, overlooked by bookkeepers. We submit, first, extracts from Flaubert's letters to Colet written prior to his writing of *Madame Bovary*.

For these extracts, we are grateful for the translation, from French to English, by Francis Steegmuller in *The Let-*

ters of Gustave Flaubert: 1830–1857, and for extracts from *Madame Bovary* from the translation by Mildred Marmor.

Aug. 8–9, 1846:
Happiness is a monstrosity; they who seek it are punished . . . Perhaps in my case it is the heart that is impotent . . . You love me so much you delude yourself . . .

. . .

Aug. 9, 1846:
. . . the grotesque aspects of love have always kept me from indulging in it. . . . But when I see you so intense, absolute in your passion, I am tempted to cry out to you: No! No! You are making a mistake not this man!

. . .

This little rose I send you. I kiss it; put it quickly in your mouth, and then—you know where.

. . .

Aug. 30, 1846:
That is everything, love of art.

. . .

Sept. 13, 1846:
Spare me; you make me giddy with your love! . . . not to consume you . . . not to drive you to despair. . . . The despondency that follows is a kind of death.

The last sentence quoted could be twisted by certain spooky bookkeepers to support Flaubert's later claim that "Madame Bovary is me." But—in this same letter Flaubert goes on to scold Colet for her love of earthly, extraneous things—those useful or agreeable. Then, in a letter two weeks later he scolds Colet for not using her intelligence in her relationship with him. Still later that year, he accuses Colet of "a correspondence that is becoming epileptic" and denies her claim that he treats her like a "woman of the lower classes."

And in his dump letter the following spring, Flaubert denounces Colet for her passionate view of their love affair, accusing his mistress of defining love as "exclusive preoccupation with the loved one; living only through him; to see, feel, experience the world only through him."

If spooky bookkeepers can't credit the input of Louise Colet to Flaubert's future portrait of the love-crazed Emma Bovary, these dudes warrant an audit on every book to which they have okayed a credit, not to mention a debit.

Flaubert, undoubtedly a creative genius, could well "paint" the finished portrait, but that he, a Realist, worked without a model for his heroine Emma Bovary—a romantic neurotic who gambled her body, then her life, in her blind hope of winning at love—doesn't wash.

Evidence again lies in writing—Flaubert's letters documenting his sworn commitment to write *only* from truth. This is backed by his lifetime personal correspondence, proof that Flaubert could never be, especially in spirit, a ghostly image for his love-starved heroine Madame Bovary. After his one brief encounter with passionate love, Flaubert recoiled at the mere thought of sinking into that morass again. Rather, there is every evidence that he used his experiences with a passionate mistress, who once enveloped him, for the spine—and the flesh—of his ill-fated romantic heroine.

Next, our audit of the numerous, and striking, similarities between Flaubert's mistress Colet and his heroine Emma Bovary:

Bovary was an adulteress many times over; ditto Colet.
Bovary lived in the provinces of southern France; ditto Colet, before her move to Paris.
Bovary was married to a wimp too stupid to figure out what games his wife was playing; ditto Colet.
Bovary had one daughter; ditto Colet.
Bovary openly defied her provincial world; ditto Colet, in the bourgeois scene of Paris.
Bovary was a flaming spendthrift married to a man who

could provide little more than life's necessities; ditto Colet.

Bovary was starved for romance but involved with a lover who choked on it; ditto Colet.

Bovary, desperate for funds, tried, without success, to borrow from her lover; double-ditto Colet.

Bovary was dumped by her one *real* lover and some minor ones along the way; ditto Colet.

Bovary is a loner feminist who identifies with the male mentality; ditto Colet.

We now submit three separate credits documented under personal notes—which, unlike her letters to Flaubert, were not destroyed—penned by Colet. First some background.

After a three year break in their relationship, and *to the week* when Flaubert decided to start writing his novel, the lovers remerge. Bookkeepers will, accurately, protest that this later merger was due solely to Colet's initiation. But, we submit, the reality of the terms of their merger later appears in *Bovary*, when Emma persists in finding love after the loss, and rejection, of her first lover.

To back this, we submit the following as a double deposit in the Louise Colet account. Colet, uninvited, visits Flaubert's home in Croisset, where she's turned away at the door, but granted—by her irate exlover—an audience later at her hotel room in Rouen. (Ah, shades of Bovary.)

Dialogue exchanged at this meeting was recorded by Colet under this scold (a prophetic echo for what will swell back from the pages of *Madame Bovary*): Flaubert greets her with sarcasm and reproach for her intrusion at his home and ". . . what he found offensive about me . . . that I was capable of such rash acts." Then, when she interjects concerns of near poverty, Flaubert slings back she (newly

widowed) should marry her protector in Paris and *then*
". . . you and I will see each other." She writes her sad, pes-
simistic response, "Oh, love profaned." (Poor, deluded Bovary.)

Following, the credit from a Flaubert letter announcing
a strategic date to his mistress—his start on *Madame Bovary*, six days after he merged again with Colet:

> September 20, 1851:
> Last night I began my novel. . . . I have had a sore
> throat . . . [in vanity I like] to think this is not due to
> fatigue. . . . And you? . . .

As a credit, Colet's note of this strategic reunion recorded the erotic scene in a carriage ride, which Flaubert
later trots out in *Bovary:*

> . . . returned in a carriage . . . the same violent emotions
> . . . said goodbye without speaking of my material situa-
> tion . . . his indifference to my poverty makes me realize
> how shallow his love is. . . . I have exactly ten francs in
> the house. . . . [Shades of poor, erotic Bovary.]

And the credit, Colet's reaction to Flaubert's letter announcing start of his novel:

> At last a note. . . . The wretchedness of my poor life can
> expect nothing . . . [but] it is better to have him back. [A
> mirror image of the sentimental Bovary.]

Now, a brief summary of some of Flaubert's with-
drawals from Colet, deposits made by her daily letters and
her investment of erotic experiences, which Flaubert re-
deposits, to his gain, in *Bovary.*

"The fuck began as I was taking her home in a *fiacre.*"
This is a Flaubert quote, from a letter written in 1862 to a
friend, describing how the Muse (his, we submit prophetic,
nickname for Colet) had *begun* to deliver herself to him. (Ad-

ditional backup for the IOU owed by Flaubert after his deposit of the carriage romp trotted out in *Bovary*.)

In his letters, Flaubert repetitiously scolds Colet for her ill-chosen reading selections and suggestions; then uses the romantic novels gobbled by Bovary as basis for her restless yearnings and later self-destruction.

Flaubert gives Bovary two real lovers, neither of whom she can possess. Colet's affair with Flaubert goes through two levels—as if there were two separate lovers: the early lover bulging with passion, and the last lover pulled back, *very* self-protective.

Flaubert makes use in *Bovary* of Emma's erotic slipper; her slipper was Colet's first gift to Flaubert.

Flaubert borrows for his *Bovary* erotic scenes played out in hotel rendezvous he had shared, over a five-year expanse, with his mistress Colet.

Now, from *Madame Bovary*, a strategic quote from the scene of the lovers' final meeting: "A demand for money, of all the winds blowing down on love, was the coldest and the most up-rooting." Shortly before this was penned, Flaubert had eased himself, as did Emma's lover, out of giving Colet financial assistance.

Flaubert dumped Colet for a final time, writing to her: "Madame: I was told [you came] to see me three times last evening. I was not in . . . [and warn you] *I shall never be in.*"

And then, the gall, in *Bovary* Flaubert seals his heroine's coming ruin with this shoddy grab from a Colet deposit. Emma's lover seals *his* dump letter using a signet ring inscribed "Amor nel Cor." Colet had given Flaubert, as a love token, a cigar holder with the identical inscription.

Finally, and fatally, Flaubert dumps Colet forever at the same time he is composing Emma's dump scene—which leads into the final tragic hours of Emma's life! (With Emma dying what use for the live Colet?)

We here insert the *solitary* IOU repaid by Flaubert to his

mistress—an extract from a letter written to Louise Colet, where he acknowledges her vaginal support during the difficult days of writing *Bovary*.

> July 22, 1852:
> I hope to be beside you (and on top of you). I need that. The end of this part of my novel has left me a little tired. I am becoming aware of it, now that the oven is beginning to cool. . . .

On this Flaubert credit, long coming, we complete our audit on the historical vaginal account of Louise Colet, with the suggestion that scholarly bookkeepers switch from their spooky entry system when it comes down to payables and receivables for vaginal private holdings.

Ghosts of a Vaginal Suicide Pact

Would a statistic that nine healthy, bonny, and sane women opted for suicide after having an intimate relationship with one man rock you? Add to this grisly total, three additional suicide attempts and the fact that one of the nine murdered six before taking her life. Would it raise a brow if we leaked that this devastating Romeo has come down in history books a far cry from the likes of a Casanova, further yet from that of a Don Juan? What if we leaked this "Romeo" holds the all-around world record for mass murder?

About to choke in disbelief? Well, take a gulp for Adolf Hitler carries the title as the world's most devastating Romeo.

Can't swallow a statistic that *twelve* times dolls took a personal vote to self-destruct for that old blabbermouth who shrieked, "My wife is Germany"? Locked in a credibility gap after a half century of Hitler bookkeeping by renowned historians and biographers? You could look at it from the bookkeeper's perspective: Hitler as a bedroom dictator is a squeak in the thunder of Hitler, Dictator of Germany *and* the roar of an earthquaking Hitler, Dictator of the World.

Or, you could take into account that an illicit squeak from the bedroom, *when recorded,* was the ruination of many a promising political career, and that the squeak of sex *and death* would have destroyed Hitler before he gained the power to destroy millions of lives.

If the future is to be safe from the horrors of yet another global madman, shouldn't we get all the facts out there on Hitler, crazed leader of a nation, one capable of selling murder and destruction to millions of sane humans? And, if accounts on Hitler were balanced to read how it came to be that in *twelve* separate incidents, women involved in his intimate life were sucked and suckered to the point of suicide, could we not hope to gain some clue to what was the secret of a hypnotic power that could sell to so many, as sanity, the insanity of annihilation—the genocide of millions of Jews?

Was Hitler too complex a personality for us to delve into his sex life? Was this a facet of his life "better left a mystery" as one of Hitler's biographers advises us? Are we, again, looking at a wash in the slush of spooky bookkeeping?

Too many questions without answers? Perhaps some of those answers lie in one question—why?

Let's pull an audit on seven—out of the nine—of Hitler's private vaginal holdings, those that slid off the sheet to the nadir point of oblivion.

Two, Eva Braun and Magda Goebbels—where books and accounts now exist—are listed here under public holdings. Still, as statistical data for Hitler's overall account on vaginal suicides, we review the following.

Eva Braun made two unsuccessful suicide attempts, in the early 1930s, first shooting herself, then popping sleeping pills, convinced that Hitler was about to dump their relationship that had started in 1932. In the end, she died by biting a cyanide capsule in the bunker alongside her lover of thirteen years—a lover who kept their relationship, till his last lost days, hidden from all but his inner circle of companions. (No one other than August Kubizek, his roommate when he was a student in Vienna, has ever claimed to be a close friend of Hitler—not even in his heyday!)

Magda Goebbels, murdered by poison—in the same bunker, hours after Hitler's death—the six children she bore to honor Hitler's dream of an Aryan Germany. That she did not love her husband, the skirt-chasing Joseph Goebbels, but was devoured by a fanatic love (which, from most accounts, did not involve sexual intercourse) for the Führer is proven by her personal decision to die by cyanide poisoning after her murder—sacrifice—of the children who existed as testimony to her fanatic bond.

Now we come to the sparse records, no books here, of the women who chose to take their lives while under the spell of sexual slavery or in the depth of depression, to escape from their loss of human dignity after forced to perform acts of sexual perversion for the masochist Hitler. (Surprised? Thought der Führer would turn up under sadistic?)

Two of these women (excluding Eva and Magda) are documented briefly—only one from the area of this audit's focus—in most Hitler biographies, leaving a remainder of five women where there are no tracks to be found in the cobwebs of spooky bookkeeping.

Hitler's suicide parade, never recorded in any depth, dates back to 1921. Due to lack of reports, the vaginal account of the leader for this ghostly parade comes down to a meager few lines: a name, Suzi Liptauer; the nationality, Viennese; residence at the time of death, Munich; where, hotel room; how, hanged herself. The why, a mixed report: one, after a night of performing acts of sexual perversion for Hitler, driven to insanity followed by suicide; two, Hitler dumped her.

The next in Hitler's suicide parade is relegated to a few lines in less than a handful of books that accompany shelves of biographies of Hitler. The year 1928; name, Maria "Mimi" Reiter; age, sixteen; hair, blond; residence, Munich; where, her home; how, attempted to hang herself, but a family member discovered her, near death, hanging by a clothesline on a door, and cut her down. Why: Hitler after a two-year love affair, sexually consummated, dumped her. As a follow-up: Did Mimi learn a lesson and avoid this SOB? Far from it. A few years later, she met with Hitler twice and in a tape-recorded interview, after the war, said, "I let him do whatever he wanted with me."

This quote is the fatal trait found in *all* of Hitler's suicidal lovers. To their ultimate peril.

We insert here a composite portrait, both physical and emotional, of Hitler's suicidal lovers who appeared, as if in uniform, over and over again in the deadly twenty-four years of Hitler's sexual life:

All lovers were blondes or of light hair; half Hitler's age; pretty, never raving beauties; personally politically unambitious except for one, whom he used for his political ambitions; athletic; nonintellectual, with one telling exception: Magda Goebbels; opposite of sadist, passive receivers sexually; lack of desire for motherhood, other than sexually frustrated Magda; feminine; liked clothes, jewelry; involved in some area of the arts, usually as dilettantes; loners; secretive; jealous; and passionate. They all appear to be, as a type, "the one-man woman." And studied from afar, all of a suicidal nature (a nature well understood by Hitler, since he, in times of deep trouble, spoke often of committing suicide, then finally in 1945, put his pistol where his mouth was—pumping a bullet in his temple; or, according to a Russian autopsy report, biting on a cyanide capsule).

Hitler had a recorded neurotic fear of syphilis—a fear so severe it brought on impotency cured only after prolonged psychiatric treatment that started in 1919. Whatever the cause, from most accounts Hitler was a sexual late bloomer for, previous to Suzi, there are no records of a woman in his life physically before the age of thirty-two. Not that opportunities were not available. His one close friend August Kubizek records in *The Young Hitler I Knew* how women were attracted to the young Hitler in the sophisticated milieu of decadent Vienna in the early 1900s:

> Adolf appealed so much to the passing ladies [foyer of opera house], in spite of his modest clothing and his cold, reserved manner in public, that occasionally one or the other of them would turn around to look at him, which . . . was considered highly improper.
>
> . . .
>
> Adolf did nothing to provoke this behavior; on the contrary, he hardly noticed the ladies' encouraging glances, or, at the most, would make an annoyed comment about them to me . . . why did he not seize these opportunities?

For those who might assume from this, and other rumors, that Hitler was a homosexual, Kubizek goes on to document that Hitler had no interest in homosexuality, though he was quite aware of it—to the point of educating his naïve friend—and took it much as a matter of fact.

That these women were beautiful, and aggressive (not at all Hitler's type) Kubizek continues:

> Was Vienna not the city of beautiful women? That this was true we needed no convincing. What was it then that held him back from doing what was normal for other young men? . . . One evening a liveried attendant handed him a note . . . he read it . . . and said, contemptuouly, "Another one . . ."
>
> . . .

I used to ask myself what the girls found so attractive about Adolf. He was certainly a well set-up young man, with regular features, but not at all what is understood by a "handsome" man . . .

. . .

Perhaps it was the extraordinarily bright eyes that attracted them. Or was it the strangely stern expression of the ascetic countenance? Or perhaps it was just his obvious indifference to the opposite sex that invited them to test his resistance.

This ascetic, stern description of Hitler was an image he projected as Führer (with Goebbels' propaganda assist) in Germany and to the outside world until his end. But the hidden Hitler, the sexual Hitler, was the antithesis of an ascetic.

And now we submit the mysterious records of Geli Raubal, Hitler's only love. But though recorded as such in most Hitler biographies, Geli remains the deepest mystery in Hitler's life to this day. Not surprising since the coverage on Hitler's only love varies in biographies from a single page to a grim, thin chapter. And her mystery is compounded, because rarely do these accounts on Geli, in life or death, jive. Other than the basics: that she was the daughter of Hitler's half-sister; blond; pretty; half Hitler's age of forty when she moved into her uncle's Munich apartment, at his request, in 1929; that the two had constant battles and were jealous of each other; that Hitler screamed back "No" from his car in the street below Geli's window after she called down a request to go to Vienna—the date, September 17, 1931; Geli was found dead in her bedroom on September 18, from a bullet in her heart; the pistol used was her Uncle Alfie's, and uncle was with his chauffeur on the road to Hamburg; that there was gossip about the Führer living with his niece; that Nazi honchos thought this gossip was a black eye for the party and that they resented Hitler's growing lack of attention to party biz, blaming Geli.

To his credit, Hitler's first biographer, Konrad Heiden, tried to get Geli's true account for his book *Der Fuehrer*, the data for which he compiled in Germany during the treacherous years of the thirties. Heiden interviewed every possible source to come up with the cause of Geli's death. When his book was published (U.S. edition, 1944), Geli's two and a half years of living, to the day of her death, with Uncle Alfie covers no more than seven pages. Unlike later biographers, Heiden wanted to get Geli's story out to the public, but in the end, all he could report from his findings was a sketchy, though gruesome, tale. And it starts with the mystery of a letter that Geli never received. Audit, if you will, this account from *Der Fuehrer*.

> At the beginning of 1929, Hitler wrote the young girl a letter couched in the most unmistakable terms. It was a letter in which the uncle and lover gave himself completely away; it expressed feelings which could be expected from a man with masochistic-coprophil inclinations . . . [the letter] fell into the hands of his landlady's son . . . it was bound to debase Hitler and make him ridiculous in the eyes of anyone who might see it.

The story of the letter, one page capable of destroying Hitler's killer future, reads like a script from a Hollywood B movie. Which makes Heiden's account of it still more creditable since, as a biographer recognized by his contemporaries, he conducted a courageous search for primary source material, working in Hitler's Germany as a known anti-Nazi. Later biographers, writing from the safety of a whipped Nazi Germany, tend to fault Heiden—as they make use of his source material—for writing histrionic history.

Analyze, and judge for yourself, some further Heiden reports of the letter that, if public, could have turned our twentieth century into a Golden Age.

With the help of a remarkable human instrument, Hitler was saved from disgrace . . . a dwarf-like eccentric named J. F. M. Rehse who . . . collected . . . in his extremely modest quarters . . . all the official decrees, political posters and leaflets. . . . In the course of years he had collected such a mass of paper that the floor of his apartment was beginning to buckle . . . he was among Hitler's early acquaintances . . . [his] partner . . . and almost friend of Hitler: Father Bernhard Stempfle . . . [was] an anti-Semitic journalist . . . an armed Bohemian in priest's robes.

Heiden goes on to report: Franz Schwarz, party treasurer (the same who burned all Nazi records before Germany fell), asked Rehse and Stempfle to buy Hitler's sadomasochistic letter back, under the pretext they must have such a precious document for their collection. The pair agreed after pulling a double blackmail; they demanded that Hitler assume Rehse's collection for a party archive and employ them as curators. This was in April 1929, a month before Geli moved into Hitler's apartment. Stempfle bought the letter: "The sum does not seem to have been small. Presumably Schwarz advanced the money from the party treasury in order to save Der Füehrer's reputation. . . . Stempfle gave the letter to Schwarz and he to Hitler. It is perhaps this service that later made Schwarz one of the most powerful, though publicly obscure, figures of the Third Reich." Father Stempfle was one of those found murdered, along with other Hitler enemies, on the "Night of the Long Knives," Hitler's first blood purge as leader of Germany. The dwarf Rehse? Lost in the passage of time.

Heiden does history, and the world, a monumental disservice when he drops, almost as an aside, this spooky bookkeeping:

In his most intimate private life he is not a sadist, but the contrary. *Here it is not intended to describe his various experiences with names and addresses;* but there is one case worth reporting because it really sheds some light on the human figure behind the gigantic image, and because it plunged Hitler the man into a real catastrophe and could perhaps be called *the* tragedy of his private life.

First emphasis ours. In truth the tragedy, for the world, was: Heiden did not get the word out, *with names and addresses*, about these masochistic experiences. In his effort to save the reputation of a few, the balance will show millions died. In private life, *the* tragedy was Geli's.

After moving into Uncle Alf's nine-room apartment, to a bedroom adjoining his, Geli became a prisoner for incest in a gilded cage—clothes, servants, trips with uncle, private singing lessons, and a chauffeur/bodyguard. Rumor has it Geli had several lovers. If so, these lovers were retaliation for a secret life as a sadistic sexual slave, and in revenge for "loving" uncle's many love affairs. Heiden reports:

> Hitler thought himself entitled to spread his affections on all sides . . . he knew no constancy or fidelity in any human relationship. His loveless core is covered with a thick foam of sentimentality and self-pity; he demands pity of his victims . . . expected his women friends to tolerate competitors . . . of which Geli could complain . . . she made other friendships . . . Hitler resisted violently. During this quarrel Geli in her despair . . . told outsiders about her relations with her uncle and the dangerous letter. Hitler was beside himself; he felt he had been betrayed as a man.

Geli wanted to leave Hitler, to stay with a friend in Vienna. Hitler, who held the pursestrings and owned the whip, refused. Next day she was found dead—bullet in her heart, twenty-three, and a mystery. The party, with the help of a pro-Nazi Minister of Justice, quashed an investigation into her suicide. Loving uncle went into retreat under protection, from a threat to commit suicide, of political aide

Gregor Strasser, another who would be wiped on that murderous night, the Night of the Long Knives.

Rumors flew: Geli was murdered by Himmler because she distracted Hitler when the party needed him most, a growing mob support to take over the leadership of Germany; Geli was pregnant after an affair with a Jewish lover and done away with to save Hitler's face; she was held prisoner by her uncle and suicide was her only escape; according to Hitler's housekeeper, she destroyed herself in the belief her uncle was having a love affair with Eva Braun.

The Why? We'll never know. The facts, never recorded, are buried in the trash of rumors. Geli's account, as private vaginal holding, is a closed file. Our audit: Bankrupt.

A Geli look-alike is recorded next in our suicide ledger. Her page in history for a Hitler suicide attempt has discreetly vanished behind the veil of secrecy that shrouds the chambers of international politics.

Geli's half-twin was Martha Dodd, daughter of William Dodd, the American ambassador in Berlin. She was a Hitler groupie, Yankee saucy and a spicy sexpot. A tempting dish to drop in the lap of a devastating Romeo who chewed up his lovers then spat them out to kiss dust. Fourteen months after Geli's suicide, Eva Braun attempted suicide by shooting herself, in the belief Hitler was about to dump her; in 1935 a second attempt was made by popping sleeping pills for the same reason. After recovery, Eva submitted to becoming the Führer's back-street mistress. Amid the waste of sex and suicide, spunky Martha Dodd caught Hitler's roving eye, much to the consternation of Hermann Göring, then head of security as leader for the Gestapo. Word was about that Martha was shifty. Wary of entrapment, Göring investigated the daughter of an ambassador who had taught history at the University of Chicago, then reputed to be a Communist breeding factory. While Hitler was pushing his act with his Geli replacement, Göring's spies searched for a possible cloak-and-dagger act that Martha might have had waiting in the wings. Before long, Göring dropped on Hitler a dossier of Martha that made the Führer see Red. Hitler didn't blink at Gestapo data claiming his Yank girlfriend had been arrested for drunkenness in Chicago, or that she rebounded a gay divorcée after a bare few months of marriage. But the drop of a Red flag—a claim Martha was a Soviet agent—and it was instant lockout.

Hitler, furious this time that he wasn't the sole role player, went all out, barring an ambassador's daughter from diplomatic receptions. Word has it, Martha slashed her wrists. What remains on her record: Martha Dodd was relieved of her American passport, tagged as a Commie in the McCarthy era, and, as a Russian agent, disappeared behind the fold of the Iron Curtain.

Number seven, out of nine, is the account of Renate Müller. Records here substantiate that after the hassle of hushing up Geli's suicide, Goebbels, responsible for the Führer's mythical ascetic image, was on a private search to find a "safe" involvement for Hitler. Better still, the solid image of a marriage to an Aryan wife, before word could leak that our Führer was not the monk of Germany—but, indeed, the sexual skunk of Germany. The woman that could play the dual role of a Hitler sex object and that of a virtuous woman to gain the approval of party leaders was a combination that would require the talents of a skillful actress.

Goebbels, as head of the National Ministry for Public Enlightenment and Propaganda (those were new days before propaganda was recognized for what it was—manufactured trash) and president of the Chamber of Culture, was in the perfect slot to find the actress who could pull off this treacherous dual role. Goebbels controlled production and publicity for all filmmaking, radio, music, visual arts, and theaters.

In this key position—to make or break—he had the pick of any actress who wanted to make it in entertainment or

the arts anywhere in Germany. With his master's key, Goebbels turned his sex life into a swinging door—until he came
up against the smashing Renate Müller, a German actress
who had built a reputation of star quality throughout Europe. Fame and stardom established, Renate could, and did,
reject Goebbels' demands for entree. As a screamer of an
egoist, Goebbels twisted Renate's rejection into one of a
woman suffocating desire to safeguard her reputation from
gossip that she was sleeping with a married man. From this
unreal twist, Goebbels decided this actress deserved to be
put under contract as the Führer's bride.

Goebbels arranged to have a screening of Renate's films
for Hitler, a renowned movie buff if films starred inviting
women. Renate intrigued the Führer, his invite went out to
join him for a weekend at Berchtesgaden. A maid at Hitler's
mountain retreat, Pauline Kohler, wrote this report of the
Müller affair after she fled Nazi Germany:

> The invitation was given and accepted . . . Renate was
> flattered . . . she was flown back to Berlin in Hitler's pri-
> vate plane . . . he sent her flowers every day . . . and
> more costly presents—diamonds and furs . . . Goebbels'
> propaganda machine went into action. Articles ap-
> peared throughout the Nazi Press praising Renate
> Müller as Germany's greatest actress. . . . She visited
> him [Hitler] at the new resplendent Chancellory. . . .
> She did not love him . . . the position he could offer her
> dazzled her imagination. Goebbels was triumphant. If
> Renate became Frau Hitler . . . Goebbels' position
> would be more than ever secure. And if she had married
> Hitler the history of the world would have been
> changed. For she was a kindly girl and would have done
> everything she could to swing Hitler round from his in-
> sane cruelty. But a Jew made it impossible.

Kohler describes in her book, *The Woman Who Lived in
Hitler's House*, written five years before Hitler's and Eva's
deaths by suicide and the collapse of Nazi Germany:

He was the only son of a Jewish millionaire . . . he met
Renate Müller, riding on a horse given her by
Hitler. . . . It was not long before she was madly in love
with him . . . there were secret meetings . . . always the
shadow of persecution hung over them . . . she persuaded her lover to leave Germany . . . together they
spent a glorious month in Paris. Hitler was forgotten
. . . the Gestapo heard of this love affair . . . they had a
complete dossier of her movements. This dossier went
in the diplomatic bag to Himmler. If it had gone to
Goebbels things might have turned out differently . . .
he has a real desire to marry Hitler off . . .

The maid continues that after Hitler saw the Gestapo's
incriminating material, he went white with fury and ordered that Renate be brought to him the moment she
crossed the frontier. Kohler and two SS men were sent to
escort Renate to Berchtesgaden under strict warning not to
discuss the Führer; and Kohler, as Muller's maid, to forget
everything the "prisoner" would discuss with her.

The maid describes Renate's fear of meeting with Hitler,
and later her apprehension, when the actress confided to her
how she survived Hitler's wrath with a plea for his loving
mercy and a vow never to meet with her Jewish lover
again—a vow she had no intention of keeping.

Before passing on to another source for this Müller audit, we quote Kohler's closing sentences for *The Woman Who
Lived in Hitler's House:*

> . . . I was glad to leave Berchtesgaden . . . to escape
> from the feverish morbidity of its atmosphere—largely
> caused by these strange love affairs. They cast over it
> the atmosphere of the expensive brothel. There was
> nothing clean and natural about it. A fog of unclean sex
> hung over it all.

In 1943, the Office of Strategic Services in the United
States commissioned psychiatrist Walter C. Langer to pre-

pare a psychological analysis of Hitler. It would be a classified secret wartime report. This report, deeply researched from every available source, was not released for publication until 1972. As a government report, it was titled "The Hitler Source Book"; in publication the title ran *The Mind of Hitler*.

Under Langer's breakdown for Masochistic Gratifications, he quotes a conversation Renate had with her film director after spending a night at the Chancellory:

> ". . . she had been sure he [Hitler] was going to have intercourse with her; that they were both undressed . . . when Hitler fell on the floor and begged her to kick him. She demurred, but he pleaded with her and condemned himself as unworthy . . . and just groveled in an agonizing manner. The scene became intolerable to her, and she finally acceded to his wishes and kicked him . . . he begged for more . . . as she continued to kick him he became more and more excited . . ."
>
> [Renate] committed suicide shortly after this experience. At this place it might be well to note that Eva Braun . . . has twice attempted suicide, Geli was either murdered or committed suicide, and Unity Mitford has attempted suicide. Rather an unusual record for a man who has had so few affairs with women.

Little did Langer know how wrong—yet how right—he was. Still, to Langer's credit, he remains the sole source to realize there was an imbalance somewhere in Hitler's "rather unusual record."

Here are various reports on why Renate Müller was found this side of death on the sidewalk three floors beneath her bedroom window: a final solution to escape her sadistic affair with the masochist Hitler; the Gestapo inprisoned her Jewish boyfriend and forced her to whip him; that Hitler visited her in a hospital after hearing of her forced beating and apologized for the actions of his Gestapo and the Gestapo retaliated and pushed her; or, she had a stroke and fell.

Without accurate data, other than her death in a hospital a few days after jumping/being pushed/falling, we close out this tragic account of Renate Müller.

Number eight in our audit is the English pro-Nazi, Unity Mitford. Unity should have been christened Disunity. This gal, despite putting on a damn good show, never got her act together, especially her suicide act. But then she was reared with a pack of eccentrics who went against the tide, backing, as liberal, stances unpopular with the majority of Englishmen. She was also taken as a sucker by Hitler for seven years.

Unity's father was the well-placed, wealthy Lord Redesdale, member of the House of Lords. He and his wife raised six free-thinking daughters and one playboy son. Unity was a Hitler groupie before she even met the Führer in Munich in 1932, when he was immediately attracted to her. Unity was, in build, unlike most women he courted. She was very tall, had an athletic build but rounded hips, flat-chested, but Aryan blond and fair. A jealous Eva Braun saw her as the threatening Valkyrie (Unity's descriptive middle name), and described Unity in her diary on May 2, 1935, under the code name Walkure (her code name for Hitler was Charlie):

> . . . he now has a substitute for me. Her name is Walkure and she looks it, including her legs. But these are the shapes that appeal to him. If that is true, he will soon have annoyed her till she gets slim unless she has Charlie's talent for thriving on worry. Worry seems to increase Charlie's appetite.

> . . .

> . . . it is mean of him not to tell me. After all he should know me well enough to realize I would never stand in his way if he should discover another romantic interest. Why should he worry about what happens to me? . . . Me, supposedly the mistress of Germany's and the

world's greatest man, have to look at him through a window!

. . .

He has so little understanding. He still makes me appear distant even when we are among his friends. Well, one makes one's own bed.

On May 28, 1935, Eva records in her diary her despair that she has lost Hitler and a hope that one word from her gallivanting Romeo would save her from the eternal sleep:

> I have just sent him a letter, one that is decisive for me. Will he consider it as important as I do? Well, I'll see. If I don't get an answer by ten o'clock tonight I'll take my twenty-five pills and lie down peacefully. Is it a sign of the terrific love which he assures me that he hasn't spoken a kind word to me for three months? Agreed, he has been busy with political problems but haven't things eased off? . . . a few kind words . . . would hardly have taken much time. I fear there is some other reason. It's not my fault. . . . Perhaps it is another woman, although I doubt it is the Walkure. But there are many others.

> . . .

> Dear God, please make it possible I see him today. Tomorrow will be too late. I have decided on thirty-five pills so as to make it dead certain this time. If he would at least have someone call up for him.

Hitler didn't call, no one called. Eva popped sleeping pills and was saved in the nick by a sister and, ironically, a Jewish doctor.

Eva was on top of it. Unity Valkyrie was not a threat to "the mistress of Germany's and the world's greatest man." Before Hitler became leader of Germany, the Valkyrie was a fetching sex object—with her aggressive manner and strong build, she looked the type to kick him around a ballroom till he saw orgasmic stars. But, once leader of a nation rising from the ashes of defeat, Hitler was desperate to build a base in the world of international politics. An ace opportunist, he used Unity Mitford's mounting passion for him to turn his well-connected English lover into his Nazi propaganda agent. Aware of the Mitfords' powerful political connections and personal friends—such as Winston Churchill and Anthony Eden—Hitler turned on his hypnotic charm. Unity, the unknowing innocent, fell into his traitor's trap.

As an agent, Unity was a hoot and a howler. In England, she greeted whomever with "Heil Hitler" and the—stick-it-up-yours—Nazi salute. She muscled into conservative circles flexing her swastika armband; at her parents English manor home, she draped unwelcome Nazi flags, and flaunted photos of herself on the arm of the Führer or his Nazi honchos.

In Germany, she was paraded in Third Reich circles as the Führer's English friend, "Lady" Mitford. In England, Unity—literally and figuratively—was no Lady (a title Hitler bestowed on her to impress his compatriots). Her reputation in Britain was a delicate balance between a groveling Nazi disgrace and a royal pain in the butt.

In 1938 under touch-base-or-run strategies to save Europe from war, Unity, in the cross-eyed belief she would become the first lady of Germany, touted to one and all the dream of an "invincible alliance between the Ruler of the Seas and the Lord of the Earth." This meshuggeneh alliance was as popular as quicksand in both nations. Hitler let Unity dig her grave, to die a traitor to her country, while he poured the foundations to put Europe in the trenches of another world war.

Difficult to fathom, but Unity was unaware she was being played as an international sucker until the very day England declared war on Germany. It was September 3,

1939, and she was in Munich. Her world collapsed with her dream of the "grand alliance" in the smoke of her Führer's attack on Poland *and* the searing awakening that Hitler had played her for—and made her—an international fool. Without a friend in sight, now an alien enemy, she courageously (with all her kookie faults, Unity was a fighter, but not, in the end, a survivor) stalked into a Nazi government office and dumped on an official's desk her signed photograph of Hitler and Nazi do-dums that she had displayed as his Anglo/Nazi patriot. She was advised to leave the country immediately.

Instead, she went to the English Gardens in Munich and pumped a bullet in her foolish head. Unity wasn't any better a shot than she was at scoring in the game of international politics. She suffered crippling brain damage. To add to her pain, she was placed under the care of Hitler's physician and locked, as an invalid, to her hospital bed.

Eva Braun, that sweetheart, sent flowers and toilet articles. Friends of Hitler's brought gifts—one a pointed Nazi emblem. Unity showed them, like a shot, where she was at. She gobbled down the Nazi emblem in a second suicide attempt. To her dismay, the Führer's doctor saved her with an emergency operation. Hitler's brain-damaged fool was shipped, through international channels, back to England in 1940. She was arrested on landing—a bedridden cripple—as a seditious element to be confined for the duration of the war. Unity died after a war that buried Germany in ruins. She died in her ruin a human vegetable.

Evidence that Hitler had set aside the role of devastating Romeo, digging his grave as world's greatest mass murderer, shows in our accounts. From 1939 to 1943, no records of lovers committing, or attempting, suicide surfaced. And, there is a weak logic that the final suicide attributed as a Hitler private vaginal holding might never have been sexually consummated. In 1943, Hitler was headed for the

171

rocks, politically and physically. The German army was fighting on all fronts and the losses were staggering. The Führer's health was deteriorating; to keep him going he was popping uppers and taking the needle under orders of his personal physician. Slowly the monkey was creeping up Hitler's back.

It was in this year of reversals and probable drug-related impotency that the brief record of Inge Ley gets tacked onto Hitler's suicide list. A striking professional ballerina, she caught the Führer's eye in the days when he could still see straight. Ley was married to a German official who was a chronic drunk. She jumped to her death in Berlin a few days before writing a possible suicide note to Hitler.

All that remains recorded—Ley's suicide, the note, destroyed—left the Führer visibly depressed. But then he had tons of rubble to depress him.

Two years later, Eva Braun and Magda Goebbels were added to Hitler's suicide ledger.

Until additional data surfaces and gets recorded in depth, Hitler's private vaginal holdings are filed *Bankrupt* and stamped *Unaccountable Receivables.*

This totals the thrust of our audit.

THE QUESTION OF VAGINAL EXPANSION IN THE TWENTY-FIRST CENTURY

In the twenty-first century, the vaginal passage will explode. In the mid-twentieth century, the vagina developed into a red star—a supergiant—burning its fuel through successive stages of expansion and contraction, fusing lighter elements into heavier ones, at an increasing pace until . . .

We all saw stars. Pal, those were heavenly days.

But with explosion comes danger of shrink.

A little shrink never hurts.

This is no small shrink, my friend. This will be cataclysmic shrink. Whambo! The furnace will be shut down, elements will collapse inward, and we will be left with a supernova, a giant dying star. No longer the star of mankind's future. The first stage—zap of input—is here; the final stage—zapping of vaginal output—is a predictable few thousand nights away.

You're predicting black holes? Isn't our world black enough as we march to the burial of a sexual revolution? Revise that forecast to a return of those red-hot stars.

What you will get is genetic star wars—a burial of human sex organs for reproduction. Let's face facts, my friend. When mankind moved out from the cave, it created family. Till recent time, there were two ways to start a family. The traditional—man impregnates woman via her vagina; after input his sperm and her egg join; baby grows in the womb; and the two become genetic parents. If that didn't work, some opted to adopt a child, many not, since they would not be their continuum, genetic parents. Then, in our twentieth century, came—after animal breeders pulled their shot to improve on nature—the zapping of a male's ejaculation into the vagina via artificial insemination, where the seminal fluid is implanted in a vagina. In animals, artificial insemination is used to improve the breed. For humans, it's another shot: Sperm, bought from a sperm bank, is used to impregnate the woman, as a replacement for the sperm of an infertile male. As a parent, the woman is the genetic link to the child, her vagina providing the passage for input and output. If the woman is infertile, or unable to carry a child, the option for a genetic link is a surrogate mother who, usually paid and bound by contract, is inseminated with the father's sperm; after her delivery, the baby is turned over to the contracting parent; as a parent, the father supplies the genetic link.

Still, a vagina remained the passage for input and output.

But the animal breeder was still out there proving to Mother Nature that I can do better than you. Better this time out meant zapping the vagina for input. Sperm and egg now meet in a saucer, join, and the fertilized egg is implanted in the uterus. In the transfer to human fertility labs, this test-tube babe takes one of two routes: one, sperm and egg of the parents do their thing in the saucer; the fertilized egg is implanted in her uterus; and after vaginal output, they are genetic parents of a test-tube baby; second route, the fertility clinic provides a host uterus, once again a woman paid and bound under contract; after labor and delivery, the contracting parents are joint genetic links. But the vagina is wiped as that strategic sluice for input—replaced by a saucer, a needle, and some scientific technology.

All work, no play. Face it pal, that's a slice of life today.

But think of tomorrow, old friend, when science will move upstairs—having "bested" the vagina—then do its job on the uterus. Sperm and egg will become one in a saucer: they will then be sucked up, deposited in an *artificial* womb; and baby will form and grow in a fishbowl; for a mother's heartbeat, the reassuring buzz of a computer; and an audience, clapping away. Not, mind you, clapping for baby, clapping, instead, each other on the back jeering, "What's *her* big deal about pregnancy? It's a snap, a pour, and a wait. Get some sperm and eggs out of the 'bank' and bring on our saucers!"

Pal, I ain't up for that shot at all.

You will not be asked, my friend. Did the wizards consult with you before they invented, then dropped, their life-saving bomb? Do they hear you now, pleading, screaming NO MORE! STOP!

No sweat. This baby will never get off their drawing boards. It'll cost the earth. One lab baby has got to run, at a min, a million bucks, while the freight for a surrogate mother is only $30 G's. True, that doesn't include the freight for attorney and court fees, if things don't jell. But then, some entrepreneur—Lloyd's of London?—will come up with a surrogate motherhood policy and everything will be jake.

As for the babes: They belong, by all that's right, with their mothers, *before* they're born. It's outright inhuman even to think of replacing the cozy womb with a sterile, well not *too* sterile, baby laboratory.

Friend, it will be baby *factories;* the lab is only for starters. As for cost, it'll drop, just like micro chips, you'll see. Of course if you're picky about genes—like genius genes—well, it's the old story, you get what you pay for. But that's their kicker. You've got the world for selection. I'm telling you, baby factories will be the way to go. Everyone loves to shop. By the end of the twenty-first century, I predict there will be a baby outlet store in every mall. Of course, if you want your kid personalized—your genes period, or some other person's genes, you know a real live copy, a clone—you're looking at specialty shops, custom orders, probably even back orders.

You are speakin' sci-fi, pal. Our world is not ready for this. Okay, I hear you, but I don't believe you. Take religion, take one: The Vatican forbids anyone, or *any thing*, to bypass the vagina when it comes to conception. Do you think zapping the womb isn't going to bring in those umpires with penalties of hell, damnation, and excommunication?

Penalties are a part of the game. We have all heard that the Vatican has decreed a new ruling: that human dignity and unity "demand that the procreation of a human person be brought about as the *fruit* of the conjugal act specific to the love between spouses . . ." all else *"morally* illicit." But where we're headed, those umps will be screaming penalty and the players won't even be in the ball park.

I gotta level, pal. I'm not locked into that route—the conception part. I say, when it comes up the pike to makin' babies, let 'em do it in saucers. It's cleaner than the backseat of a car and the sheets in a lot from of motels. Let the little bugger get a clean start, then pop him/her in a real uterus till it's time to slide down the ole vagina pipeline. That route saves a lot from headaches. You can pick your slot and leave the driving to us.

Is that your image for the vagina of the future? The vagina as a sex object . . . period! You're a raving sexist.

Buddy, this is *not* a sexist image. It's equal rights. The penis has been the sex symbol—period—since year one. It's time the vagina got its share of the spotlight. As a sex organ, the vagina was locked in with conception. Set it free and the vagina will be right up there sharing top billing with the penis as a sex symbol. The problem is . . . well, the vagina's got no history as an image. Vulvas, you know, are all over the place—from the cover to the centerfold—but the vagina's been invisible forever.

You have been looking with blinders on, my friend. Check out the book, *The Power of the Symbol*, where the facade and the interior of Gothic churches are defined as symbols for the female genitalia and sex organ. As you said, vulvas are all over the place, so peek into this sacred site:

Many church doors are patterned after the vulva to such an extent that each anatomical part of the vulva has a part . . . a small opening inside the walls on each side of the vestibule, which in the vulva is the opening duct of the Bartholin glands, which secretes a lubricant in sexual excitement . . . [the] holy water fonts on each side . . . for worshipers to anoint themselves before proceeding . . . the inner door of the vestibule of the church (labia minora) leads into the hallway (vagina), which extends inward to the altar (uterus or womb), from which paths lead to each side of the womb (Fallopian tubes) to a vestry or study (ovaries).

That is one grand vision, pal.

Wait till you check out the input and output:

From here a priest in female attire (an ovule) goes to the altar (uterus) to admit a new applicant for membership (a sperm), who is immersed or sprinkled with water (amniotic fluid) and then is sent, on his way out, through the same structures symbolically that he passed through when he first came into the world, following which he can say, "I was born again". . .

And then there is the fifteenth-century masterpiece hanging in the Louvre—the vagina restricted to a solo output minus an input—painted by Leonardo da Vinci.

Tell me it's the Mona Lisa and you're due for a sock in the eye—both eyes. That painted lady has been box office mysterious for her fuckin' smile and her fuckin' look for centuries. And Leonardo, maybe because he was a homosexual, had the laugh on all of us because Mona has some fuckin' secret nobody knows about.

The painting I'm referring to celebrates another vaginal secret. For a clue, take in a quote from the art historian H. W. Janson describing the painting, an altar panel—true *his* vision did not expand for vaginal imagery—but picture, if you will:

> Here the figures emerge from the semidarkness of the grotto, enveloped in a moisture-laden atmosphere that delicately veils their forms. This fine haze . . . lends a peculiar warmth and intimacy to the scene. It also creates a beautiful dreamlike quality, and makes the picture seem a poetic vision rather than an image of reality pure and simple . . . mysterious in many ways . . . the secluded, rocky setting . . . the plant life, carefully chosen . . . all hint at symbolic meanings that are somehow hard to define . . . few pictures cast a more enduring spell.

With all his moxie, how come this Janson was wearing blinders same as me?

We have all been wearing blinders when it comes to a history of the vagina. Science never even examined it, anatomically, until the twentieth century. But Leonardo did; proof lies in his notes and sketchbooks, with pages on embryology, an anatomical sketch of humans in coitus, and a drawing, possibly the first ever made from dissection, of the unborn babe in the womb.

Okay, Leonardo knew his beans. What did he call his no-input vaginal portrait?

"The Virgin of the Rocks."

Swell, pal. Just the sex image we're gonna be looking for in the dynamite of the twenty-first century—*a* Virgin staring down *a* stack of penis-shaped rockets.

That was the image of the sacred vagina in Leonardo's time, and centuries before. The ideal virginal vagina: the Virgin poised in her sensuous grotto, encircled by an angel, a saint, and her pure babe. At the entrance to her grotto, huge phallic rocks stand, isolated, but threatening. If Leonardo were painting today, I wonder what would be his vision of a modern vagina to paint. In the huge shadow of a complex future, would we recognize an image for the vagina of the twenty-first century?

Hate to lay it on you, buddy, we have today's image. The Femme Fatale. Now, let *me* take my shot with a quote. I met this writer, Eugene Wildman, in a saloon—you know O'Rourke's—he teaches English at the University of Illinois in Chicago. He lays on me he's been a lover of enchantresses since he first got rollin'. As he was a with-it guy, I asked him what was up.

Nobody's up. Picture, if you will, this sick piece for an historical slice:

> The enchantress of today differs from her sisters of the past. Prowess and power provide the basis for her appeal. Yet this more recent image is changing, because the state of the art enchantress is becoming what she was in the past, the femme fatale in the most literal sense. The AIDS epidemic returns to women the role they had before, that of a distant object of desire. It is too possible to die for sex. So women will, once again, be seen as dangerous, perhaps fatal temptresses.

179

You memorized that quote. Will your reconnaissance of vaginal secrets ever cease?

I also bought a gross of rubbers—celibacy (if it's not a fairy tale) is okay for priests, but the life of abstinence is for saints. When our Surgeon General came out with the prediction that 100 million could die of AIDS worldwide by the turn of the century, only a fool would not put on his helmet before he enters the trenches. So I'm saluting the General and wearin' two per shot.

That's a shot in the right direction.

Who you?

Venus Rising.

I love it. Do we call you Venus or Rising for short?

Venus, for a start, and I'll call you, for a start, my friend, and you, my pal. Today, we are all tagged Fatale till V day when the vaccine comes through—a day our Surgeon General says won't be in the twentieth century—and we've won our battle with AIDS.

You're right on about Fatale. Leery, aren't we? Last year—last month—this conversation might well have been pillow talk. *C'est la vie!* Then—*El morte!* A toast to the twenty-first century. How will we pass the time, Venus?

How about probing for some answers on who has charge of copulation?

Take the first poke Venus.

Why, since science persists in berating us that sex is never safe, have those wizards yet to come up with—for nigh onto five centuries—an acceptable, better yet, a desirable condom? We're not asking—heavenly days!—for something, far-out, such as erotic. Something surefire safe, pleasurable on both ends, would seem a small thing, with all their magic, to pull out of a rubber bag. Instead, scientific energy is being spent, in England, to invent a method for males to become pregnant.

That'll be a bust.

And, in Japan, they are working on a birth-control pill for men. My question: Will the penis turn green?

Green! Bite your tongue! What gamy revenge is this? You would have the penis exchange its rosy blush for a gangrenous green?

No. A flashy green, to signal to us gals it's really safe to go.

We get the point. Next question.

If genetic wizard splitters in the United States are now inserting into embryos the growth-regulating genes of rats and humans to create giant mice . . .

Giant mice! How big is giant?

Two and a half times in size.

Rats! Still, it could have been man-size.

Don't count your chickens—well, let's say pigs and sheep, where the human gene is inserted into their embryos.

How gigantic are these pigs? Sheep are silly anyway.

Five foot in height. And they're patented.

Those hogs! They didn't grab enough zapping seminal input, and then vaginal input, and now chomping on vaginal output. Now, they're fuckin' around with our genes.

Perhaps that's not our Venus' point. Could it be a hope that the genetic wizards will eventually zero in on the human penis and make bigger for me and better for her?

My pal, bigger is not always better. Evolution proves that—and if the vagina had a voice you would hear "Amen" in addition to "Ah men!" But the vagina has no voice and her output for evolution is under the gun of genetic engineers. As before, with reproduction "improvements," the genetic games start in the animal world. The evolutionary threat from biotechnology is laid out by the director for the study of Animal Protection, Michael W. Fox:

> Proponents of genetic engineering argue that man has,
> through selective breeding, already modified farm ani-

mals to boost production. They also argue that these new techniques of gene transfer between species are not fundamentally different from the old method of selective breeding. This ignores there are genetic barriers between animal species that prevent interbreeding and the exchange of genes from one species with those from another. This is one of Nature's rules that may be imprudent for us to ignore.

May be! The question is: Evolution labored 200,000 years—according to a "molecular clock" used as a method of determining when various related species diverged in the course of evolution, to produce "Eve"—delivering a maternal ancestor for every human being living today. Will "Eve's" 200,000 years of delivery be blown away in the creation of a new Eve that will rise out of a genetic test tube?

Venus, what about "Adam"—the paternal ancestor of every human being, past and present?

There is no "Adam" according to the genetic biologists working from the molecular clock. Sperm lacks mitochondrial genes, not so the woman's egg, which has thousands. We all get our mitochondria only from our mothers. Therefore, "Eve" is *the* source to trace our genealogical family tree.

You're steamed about a test-tube "Eve"? Venus, where are *you* coming from these days? Those snaky wizards just zapped "Adam"!

What a slash in the rib, right poppa? So what action do we take to drive all genetic snakes out of *our* "Garden of Eden"? They're moving in on our turf, daddy-oh.

Unite, lay down our law and zap their funding. Put all dough available into researching condoms. A Nobel, if it comes up erotic. And, when those wizards have accomplished that, let 'em solve the enigma of a vaginal symbol, a sign to light our way in the passage of the twenty-first century. Let evolution do nature's job on earth. If we're gonna meet up with aliens let 'em come in outer space.

Nature provided the vaginal symbol from the start, my friend. Take a read on the anatomical drawing of a female's genital area. You see at the bottom, a dot, the tiny clitoris; above a staff, the vagina; over all, the hook, a uterus. In mass, this figure reads: the mark of the unknown—a question mark. At the center of this mark—the vagina, the core. In the twenty-first century, the penis, via the phallic symbol of a spacecraft, will blaze a trail to explore the unknown. Waiting to receive the penis, exploding perpetual stars, will be the vagina—the unknown space—the symbol for all mystery. Fathomless.

A universe.

BIBLIOGRAPHY

Anonymous. *My Secret Life*. New York: Grove Press, 1966.

Anonymous. *The Slang of Venery*. Unpublished manuscript, 1916.

Attenborough, D. *The Living Planet*. Boston: Little, Brown, 1984.

Azimov, I. *Azimov's Guide to the Bible*. New York: Avenel Books, 1981.

Barraclough, G. *The Christian World*. New York: Harry Abrams, 1980.

Berger, C. B. *Our Phallic Heritage*. New York: Greenwich Book Publishers, 1966.

Brake, M., ed. *Human Sexual Relations*. New York: Pantheon Books, 1982.

Braudel, F. *The Perspective of the World*, vol. 3. S. Reynolds, trans. New York: Harper & Row, 1979.

———. *The Structures of Everyday Life*, vol. 1. S. Reynolds, trans. New York: Harper & Row, 1981.

Bullock, A. *Hitler: A Study in Tyranny*. New York: Harper & Bros., 1962.

Bullough, V. L. *Sexual Variance in Society and History*. Chicago: University of Chicago Press, 1976.

Bullough, V., and B. Bullough. *Sin, Sickness, and Sanity: A History of Sexual Attitudes*. New York: New American Library, 1977.

Calderone, M. S., and E. W. Johnson. *The Family Book About Sexuality*. New York: Harper & Row, 1981.

Cavendish, R., ed. *Legends of the World*. New York: Schocken Books, 1982.

De Beauvoir, S. *The Second Sex*. New York: Vintage Books, 1974.

De Sade, Marquis. *The 120 Days of Sodom and Other Writings*. Compiled and translated by A. Wainhouse and R. Seaver. New York: Grove Press, 1966.

Devereaux, C. *Venus in India*. Los Angeles: Holloway House Publishing Co., 1967.

Diagram Group, The. *Sex: A User's Manual*. New York: Berkley Books, 1983.

————. *Woman's Body: An Owner's Manual*. New York: Bantam Books, 1981.

Dickinson, R. L., and L. A. Beam. *A Thousand Marriages*. Baltimore: Williams & Wilkins Co., 1931.

Dictionary of the Holy Bible, for General Use in the Study of the Scriptures. New York: American Tract Society, 1859.

Douglas, N., and P. Slinger. *Sexual Secrets: The Alchemy of Ecstasy*. New York: Destiny Books, 1979.

Dunkell, S. *Lovelives*. New York: Signet Books, 1978.

Durant, W., and A. Durant. *The Story of Civilization*, vols. 1–11. New York: Simon & Schuster, 1954–1975.

Ellis, A., and A. Abarbanel, eds. *The Encyclopedia of Sexual Behavior*. New York: Jason Aronson, 1973.

Ellis, A. *Sex Without Guilt*. New York: Lyle Stuart, 1958.

Ellis, H. *Psychology of Sex*, 2nd ed. New York: Harcourt, Brace & Jovanovich, 1966.

Ellis, H. *Studies in Psychology of Sex*, vols. 1 and 2. San Diego: Academy Press, 1970.

The Encyclopaedia Britannica. Chicago: Encyclopaedia Britannica Inc., 1974.

Finch, B. E., and H. Green. *Contraception Through the Ages*. London: Peter Owen, 1963.

Fisher, H. *The Sex Contract*. New York: William Morrow & Co., 1982.

Flaubert, G. *The Letters of Gustave Flaubert: 1830–1857*. F. Steegmuller, trans. Cambridge, MA: The Belknap Press of Harvard University Press, 1980.

Flaubert, G. *Madame Bovary*. M. Marmur, trans. New York: New American Library, 1979.

Foucault, M. *The History of Sexuality*, vol. 1. New York: Vintage House, 1980.

Francoen, R. T. *Utopian Motherhood: New Trends in Human Reproduction*. Garden City, NY: Doubleday & Co., 1970.

Frazer, Sir J. G. *The Golden Bough*, vol. 1, abridged. New York: Macmillan Publishing Co., 1963.

Freedman, H. *The Sex Link*. New York: M. Evans & Co., 1977.

Freud, S. *Three Essays on the Theory of Sexuality.* New York: Basic Books, 1981.

Fryer, P. *The Birth Controllers.* New York: Stein and Day, 1965.

Gibbon, E. *The Decline and Fall of the Roman Empire.* New York: Wise & Co., 1943.

Girouard, Mark. *The Return to Camelot.* New Haven: Yale University Press, 1981.

Goldberg, I. *The Sacred Fire.* New York: Alfred A. Knopf, 1930.

Grant, M. *From Alexander to Cleopatra.* New York: Charles Scribner's Sons, 1982.

Grayzel, S. *A History of the Jews.* New York: Mentor Books, 1968.

Green, S. *The Curious History of Contraception.* New York: St. Martin's Press, 1971.

Gun, E. N. *Eva Braun: Hitler's Mistress.* New York: Meredith Press, 1968.

Heiden, K. *Der Fuehrer.* Boston: Houghton Mifflin, 1944.

Heiman, J., L. LoPiccolo, and J. LoPiccolo. *Becoming Orgasmic: A Sexual Growth Program for Women.* Englewood Cliffs, NJ: Prentice-Hall, 1976.

Himes, N. E. *Medical History of Contraception.* New York: Gamut Press, 1963.

The Hindu Art of Love (Ananga Ranga). London: Castle Books, 1969.

Hite, S. *The Hite Report: A Nationwide Study of Female Sexuality.* New York: Dell Publishing Co., 1979.

Hoffmann, H. *Hitler Was My Friend.* London: Burke Publishing Co., Ltd., 1955.

Hollander, X. *The Happy Hooker.* New York: Dell Publishing Co., 1982.

The Holy Bible, authorized King James Version. Nashville: The Gideons International, 1974.

Hopper, R. J. *The Early Greeks.* New York: Barnes & Noble, 1976.

Hunt, M. M. *The Natural History of Love.* New York: Alfred A. Knopf, 1981.

Infield, G. B. *Eva and Adolf.* New York: Ballantine Books, 1974.

Janson, H. W. *History of Art.* New York: Harry N. Abrams, 1968.

Jones, E. *The Life and Work of Sigmund Freud.* New York: Basic Books, 1961.

The Kama Sutra of Vatsyayana. Sir R. Burton, trans. New York: Berkley Books, 1984.

Kassorla, Dr. I. *Nice Girls Do—and now you can too!.* Los Angeles: Stratford Press, 1984.

Kavaler, L. *A Matter of Degree*. New York: Harper & Row, 1981.

Kiefer, O. *Sexual Life in Ancient Rome*. New York: Barnes & Noble, 1962.

Kinsey, A. C., W. Pomeroy, C. E. Martin, and P. H. Gebhard. *Sexual Behavior of the Human Female*. Philadelphia: W. B. Saunders, 1953.

Knauth, P., ed. *The Illustrated Encyclopedia of the Animal World*. New York: The Danbury Press, 1971.

Kohler, Pauline. *The Woman Who Lived in Hitler's House*. New York: Sheridan House, 1940.

Krich, A., ed. *The Sexual Revolution*. New York: Dell Books, 1963.

Kruck, W. E. *Looking for Dr. Condom*. University, AL: University of Alabama Press, 1981.

Krueger, K. *I Was Hitler's Doctor*. New York: Biltmore Publishing Co., 1943.

Kubizek, A. *The Young Hitler I Knew*. E. V. Anderson, trans. New York: Tower Publications, 1954.

Ladas, A., B. Whipple, and J. D. Perry. *The G Spot and Other Recent Discoveries About Human Sexuality*. New York: Holt, Rinehart and Winston, 1982.

Langer, W. *The Mind of Hitler*. New York: New American Library, 1972.

Lanson, L. *From Woman to Woman*. New York: Pinnacle Books, 1981.

Lehrman, R. *Masters and Johnson Explained*. New York: Playboy Paperbacks, 1970.

"M." *The Sensuous Woman*. New York: Lyle Stuart, 1969.

Malinowski, M. *Sex, Culture, and Myth*. London: Hart-Davis, 1963.

———. *The Sexual Life of Savages*. New York: Harcourt, Brace & World, 1929.

Manvell, R., and H. Fraenkel. *Inside Adolf Hitler*. New York: Pinnacle Books, 1973.

Marcus, S. *The Other Victorians*. New York: Meridan Books, 1974.

Marvels and Mysteries of Our Animal World. Pleasantville, NY: The Reader's Digest Association, 1964.

Masson, J. M. *The Assault on Truth: Freud's Suppression of the Seduction Theory*. New York: Farrar, Straus and Giroux, 1984.

Masters, W. H., and V. E. Johnson. *Human Sexual Response*. Boston: Little, Brown & Co., 1966.

———. *The Pleasure Bond*. New York: Bantam Books, 1980.

McMullen, Roy. *Mona Lisa*. Boston: Houghton Mifflin, 1975.

Mead, M. *Male and Female*. New York: Morrow Quill Paperbacks, 1977.

Meyer, J. J. *Sexual Life in Ancient India*. New York: Barnes & Noble, 1953.

Moore, J. C. *Love in Twelfth-Century France*. Philadelphia: University of Pennsylvania Press, 1972.

Morris, D. *Animal Days*. New York: Perigord Press, 1979.

———. *The Naked Ape*. New York: McGraw-Hill, 1967.

Morris, I. *The Pillow Book of Sei Shonagon*. New York: Penguin Books, 1971.

Murphy, E. *Great Bordellos of the World*. London: Quartet Books, 1983.

The New Larousse Encyclopedia of Animal Life. New York: Bonanza Books, 1980.

Newman, F. X., ed. *The Meaning of Courtly Love*. Albany, NY: State University of New York Press, 1968.

O'Brien, M. *All the Girls*. New York: Fawcett Press, 1982.

O'Faolain, J., and Martines, L., eds. *Not In God's Image*. New York: Harper & Row, 1973.

Opie, I., and P. Opie. *The Oxford Dictionary of Nursery Rhymes*. Oxford: Oxford University Press, 1951.

Parrinder, G., ed. *World Religions*. New York: Facts on File, 1983.

Partridge, E. *Origins*. New York: Macmillan Publishing Co., 1983.

Payne, R. *The Life and Death of Adolf Hitler*. New York: Popular Library, 1973.

The Perfumed Garden of the Shaykh Nefzawi. Sir R. Burton, trans. New York: Dell Publishing, 1982.

Pfeiffer, J. E. *The Creative Explosion*. New York: Harper & Row, 1982.

Pomeroy, S. B *Goddesses, Whores, Wives, and Slaves*. New York: Schocken Books, 1975.

Quaife, G. R. *Wanton Witches and Wayward Wives*. New Brunswick, NJ: Rutgers University Press, 1979.

Raley, P. E. *Making Love*. New York: Dial Press, 1976.

Rawson, H. A. *A Dictionary of Euphemisms and Other Doubletalk*. New York: Crown Publishers, 1981.

Reese, W. L. *Dictionary of Philosophy and Religion*. Atlantic Highlands, NJ: Humanities Press, 1980.

Ropp, R. S. *Sex Energy*. New York: Delta Books, 1969.

Sanger, W. *The History of Prostitution*. New York: Eugenics Publishing Co., 1937.

188

Schulberg, L. *Historic India*. New York: Time-Life Books, 1968.

Scott, G. R. *Curious Customs of Sex & Marriage*. London: Torchstream Books, 1953.

Seligmann, K. *Magic, Supernaturalism and Religion*. New York: Pantheon Books, 1971.

Shipley, J. T. *Dictionary of Word Origins*. New York: The Philosophical Library, 1945.

Spears, R. A. *Slang and Euphemism*. Middle Village, NY: Jonathan David Publishers, 1981.

Stebbins, G. *Darwin to DNA, Molecules to Humanity*. New York: W. H. Freeman and Co., 1982.

Tannahill, R. *Sex in History*. New York: Stein and Day, 1980.

Taylor, G. R. *Sex in History*. New York: Harper Torchbooks, 1970.

Terres, J. K. *The Audubon Society Encyclopedia of North American Birds*. New York: Alfred A. Knopf, 1980.

Thompson, P. *The Edwardians*. New York: Paladium Books, 1975.

Toland, J. *Adolf Hitler*. New York: Ballantine Books, 1977.

Toynbee, A. J. *A Study of History*. New York: Oxford University Press, 1947.

Trevor-Roper, H. R. *The Last Days of Hitler*. New York: Macmillan Publishing Co., 1947.

Walker, B. *The Woman's Encyclopedia of Myths and Secrets*. San Francisco: Harper & Row, 1983.

Wallace, I. *The Nympho and Other Maniacs*. New York: Simon and Schuster, 1971.

Wallace, I., A. Wallace, D. Wallechinsky, and S. Wallace. *The Intimate Sex Lives of Famous People*. New York: Delacorte Press, 1981.

Wallace, R. A. *How They Do It*. New York: Morrow Quill Paperbacks, 1980.

Walters, R. G., ed. *Primers for Prudery*. Englewood Cliffs, NJ: Prentice-Hall, 1974.

Warner, M. *Alone of All Her Sex*. New York: Vintage Books, 1976.

Webb, P. *The Erotic Arts*. New York: Farrar, Straus and Giroux, 1983.

Wendt, H. *The Sex Life of Animals*. New York: Simon and Schuster, 1965.

Young, W. *Eros Denied: Sex in Western Society*. New York: Grove Press, 1964.

INDEX

191

insects, 22 — 23, 79
Intimate Sex Lives of Famous People, 86
Isis, 40
Israel, ancient, 40 — 41
Italy, 48, 52, 65, 67, 109

Jack and Jill, 117
Jade Stalk (penis), 81 — 82
James, Jennifer, 61
Janson, H.W., 178
Japan, 181
Jesus Christ, 45 — 46, 101 — 102
John, "the Golden Mouth," 101
Johnson, Virginia E. (see Masters and Johnson)
Jones, Emmie Marie, 24 — 25
Journal of American Medical Society, The, 143 — 144
Joyce, James, 91
Justin Martyr, Saint, 101
Justinian I, Emperor of Byzantium, 46 — 47

Kama Sutra (Vatsyayana), 3, 79
King of Macedon, 44
Kinsey, Alfred C., 31 — 33, 113 — 114
kissing, 31 — 33
knights, 106 — 107
Kohler, Pauline, 165 — 166
Koop, C. Everett (see U.S. Surgeon General)
Kubizek, August, 156, 158 — 159

labia, 2, 196
Lady Chatterley's Lover (Lawrence), 90 — 91
Lamina, 44
Lancelot, 122
Langer, Walter C., 166 — 167
Lanson, Lucienne, 33
Lawrence, D.H., 90 — 91
Layon, Marie, 110
Leonardo da Vinci, 178 — 179
Leontion, 42
Letters of Gustave Flaubert, The

(Steegmuller), 148 — 149
Ley, Inge, 172
lions, 27, 28 — 29
Liptauer, Suzi, 156
lizards, 20, 24, 30
Louis VII, King of France, 105 — 106
Louvre, 178
Love in the East, 37
Love Letters (Aristaenetus), 42
Luke, Saint and Apostle, 45 — 46
Luther, Martin, 108

Madame Bovary (Flaubert), 146 — 154
Magnus, Albert, 115
major labia, 2, 33
Male Member, The (Schwartz), 125, 137
Manhattan, 68
Mann, Jonathan, 74
mantis, 23
Mare, The (medium vagina), 3 — 4
Marmor, Mildred, 149
Maro, 61
marriage, 36, 76, 94 — 100, 103, 176
Mary Magdalene, 45 — 46
masochism, 156, 160, 167
Masons, 45
Masters and Johnson, 2, 4, 19, 32, 35 — 36
Masters, William H. (see Masters and Johnson)
masturbation, 33 — 38, 112, 122
mating habits, non-human, 26 — 30
menstrual blood, 115
Mexico, 24
mice, 181
Middle Ages, 46 — 47, 75
Middle East, 40, 41, 45 — 46, 97
Mind of Hitler, The (Langer), 166 — 167
minor labia, 2, 33, 37, 177
mistresses, 48

Mitford, Unity, 167 — 171
molecular clock, 182
Mona Lisa, 178
monks, 4, 51
monogamy, 109, 125, 143
Moses, 40 — 41, 102
Mount of Venus, 2
Muller, Renate, 165 — 168
multiorgasmic, 72 — 73, 78, 79, 80 — 83
Munich, 156, 157, 159, 168, 171
music, 32
My Secret Life (Anon.), 88 — 90

nannies, 121
National Academy of Sciences, 75
Natural History of Love, The (Hunt), 107
Nebuchadnezzar, 40, 102
Nefzawi, Shaykh, 5 — 6
New England, 111
New Larousse Encyclopedia, 28
New York Times, 74 — 75
Night of the Long Knives, 161, 163
non-sexual conception, 24 — 25, 93, 101 — 102, 191 — 196
non-sexual reproduction, 24, 93
Normany, 106
nymphomania, 62

O'Brien, Martin, 61
octopus, 21
odors, 27, 30, 32
oral sex, 31 — 32, 144
orgasmic phase, 19
orgasms, 71 — 73, 77 — 91, 123
Original Sin, 103
Origin of Evil, 103
O'Rourke's saloon, 179
Osiris, 40
ova, 174 — 175, 177, 182
ovaries, 177
Oxford English Dictionary, The Compact Edition of, 18

Padma dkar-po, 4
passive/receiver, 126

Pearl, Cora, 61
pelvis, 124
penis (human, male sex organ), 2, 34 — 38, 69, 72, 80 — 82, 86 — 90, 93 — 94, 97, 103, 113, 181, 183
penis (non-human), 21, 23, 24, 28, 30
penis envy, 34
Pennsylvania, 111
Perfumed Garden, The (Nefzawi), 4 — 6, 83
Pericles, 44
Persia (Iran), 97
Peter Simon, Saint, 101 — 102
petting, 31
phallic symbolism, 93, 177, 179, 183
Phryne, 43 — 44
pigs, 181
Pill, the (oral contraception), 92, 113, 125, 181
Pincus, Gregory, 113
Platonic, 98, 99
Poland, 171
Pope Siricius, 102
popes, 47, 48
pornography, 32
Power of the Symbol, The, 177 — 178
pregnancy, 92, 125, 174, 180
premenstrual phase, 32
Presley, Elvis, 86, 124 — 125, 127
primitive time, 2 — 3, 64, 92 — 95, 174
procreation, 99 — 103, 176
prostitutes, descriptions, 54 — 59
Prostitutes Rights Contingent, 62
prostitution, 39 — 62, 96 — 97, 143
Puritan, 111 — 112

radio, 127
rats, 181
Raubal, Geli, 159 — 163
Redesdale, Lord, 168

195

U.S. Surgeon General, 73 — 74, 75, 125, 180
University of Chicago, 163
University of Illinois, 179
University of Miami, 144
uterus, 18, 175, 176, 177, 183

vaginal biological development, 20 — 21
vaginal fluids, 3 — 4, 19, 32, 67, 81 — 83, 177
vaginal size, 3 — 6, 19, 78
vaginal symbols, 177 — 179, 182 — 183
Vatican, 176
Vatsyanna Mallanage, 80
Venus, 62, 180 — 182
Venus statuettes, 2
Victorian Age, 63 — 67, 121 — 123
Vienna, 156, 158 — 159, 162
Virgin Mary, 24, 100 — 102
virginity, 92 — 93, 101 — 102, 103 — 104, 114, 121, 179
virgin sacrifice, 92 — 93
virgo (virgin), 103
Voltaire, 110
vulva, 3 — 6, 18, 97, 109, 110, 177

Wales, 111 — 112
Wallace, Robert A., 22
Washington D.C., 126, 143
Washington Post, 74, 126, 143
Webster's New International Dictionary (1956), 37
whales, 22
Wildman, Eugene, 179
Wilmot, John, Earl of Rochester, 87
Wolff, Dr. Sheldon, 74
Woman to Woman (Lanson), 33
Woman Who Lives in Hitler's House (Kohler), 165
womb, 115, 174 — 176, 177, 179
World Health Organization, 74
World War II, 31, 123, 171 — 172

yoni, 3 — 4
Young Hitler, The (Kubizek), 158 — 159

zebras, 27
zoos, 76
Zoroastrianism, 97 — 98, 99